RECOVERING

FROM DIVORCE

. . .AND THE HORSE YOU

RODE IN ON!

BY
BILL WEAR, JR.

ILLUSTRATED BY
JACK WIENS

AUDIO CASSETTES BY THE AUTHOR

"The Art Of Healing Yourself"
"The Meditation Process--How To Meditate"

For information on audio cassette tapes, books and seminar schedules for Bill and Sheila Wear, please mail a self-addressed, stamped envelope to: Insight Productions, P.O. Box 10826, Springfield, MO 65808-0826.

Written by Bill Wear, Jr.
Illustrated by Jack Wiens.

FIRST EDITION

Printed and bound in the United States of America.

Published by:
INSIGHT PRODUCTIONS
P.O. BOX 10826
SPRINGFIELD, MISSOURI 65808-0826

DEDICATION

This book is dedicated to everyone who has experienced divorce
or relationship challenges
and to the professionals who help their clients
"walk through the shadow of" divorce.

I especially dedicate this work to my wife, Sheila,
whose love, encouragement and support helped create this book.

ACKNOWLEDGEMENTS

I gratefully acknowledge:

All my divorce and counseling clients who inspired me to write this book;

Jack Wiens for his terrific illustrations and encouragement;

Brenda Walker for her patience, creativity and willingness to help;

Monica Sowards for her input, proofreading and encouragement;

Karen Colton for her suggestions and editing skills;

My dad, Bill Wear, Sr., Jim Sharp and Karsten E. "Bad Boy" Bredesen
for helping give me the time and energy to write the book
by taking up the slack at the office and for their encouragement;

My mom, Julie Wear, for her experience, strength and hope and
Sheila, Roadie and Champ for their love and support.

TABLE OF CONTENTS

IV. EMOTIONAL AND SPIRITUAL HEALING

V. WORKING THE 12 STEPS

Based upon my experience as a divorce attorney, marriage and family counselor, minister, divorce mediator and divorce participant, odds are that your divorce will be the most painful experience you will ever encounter. Divorces are emotionally charged with levels of emotional conflict that range from passive aggression to outright homicide. Many times only one spouse wants out of the marriage (at least at first). Spouses find it difficult, if not impossible, to remain civil to one another, and in some instances attorney fees and court costs leave the divorced couple in debt. The conflict generated by the legal system, as each spouse retains his or her own "hired gun," escalates the already volatile emotional environment in which spouses find themselves. And remember, these two people used to be in love with each other. In the typical divorce case, you will find two former lovers who now despise each other, who feel confused, hurt, upset, frightened and guilty and whose children remind them of the other spouse. The spiritual and emotional costs of divorce are staggering.

The warfare of divorce leaves casualties. Divorcing spouses suffer massive doses of emotional pain. Parents watch helplessly as emotional warfare engulfs their children: children who are at risk of repeating the conflict and divorce behavior modeled by their parents; children who will find it difficult, if not impossible, to trust their parents, themselves, other people or God; children who will experience fits of depression, rage and guilt; and children who will take their own lives or turn to drugs and alcohol to ease their pain.

Divorce leaves behind heartaches and suffering that are less visible: the pain the couple's friends go through; the suffering each family undergoes as one of their own walks through the divorce experience and future relationship difficulties the divorcing spouses will encounter that will breed even more pain for themselves, their children, their families and friends. The emotional pain of anger, fear, guilt and sadness can consume the entire family.

This book is about recovering from the emotional and spiritual devastation of divorce. "The horse you rode in on" is a metaphor representing your past experiences -- the good, the bad and the ugly. Marriages die because we are unskilled at meeting our own needs while involved in relationships. If "the horse you rode in on" (your past) did not prepare you to adequately meet the tests of a marriage relationship -- join the club. The following pages will assist you in healing the wounds of your divorce AND help you and your horse find happier trails that will lead to healthier relationships and a more joyful life.

> *But it is from our twisted relations with family, friends, and society at large that many of us have suffered the most. We have been especially stupid about them. The primary fact that we fail to recognize is our total inability to form a true partnership with another human being. Our egomania digs two disastrous pitfalls. Either we insist upon dominating*

the people we know, or we depend upon them far too much. If we lean too heavily on people, they will sooner or later fail us, for they are human, too, and cannot possibly meet our incessant demands. In this way our insecurity grows and festers. When we habitually try to manipulate others to our own willful desires, they revolt, and resist us heavily. Then we develop hurt feelings, a sense of persecution, and a desire to retaliate. As we redouble our efforts at control, and continue to fail, our suffering becomes acute and constant. We have not once sought to be one in family, to be a friend among friends, to be a worker among workers, to be a useful member of society. Always we tried to struggle to the top of the heap, or to hide underneath it. This self-centered behavior blocked a partnership relation with any one of those about us. Of true brotherhood we had small comprehension. (1)

I. INTRODUCTION

THE NUMBERS

Divorce and family statistics in our country are downright depressing. Approximately fifty percent of all "first" marriages are doomed from the start. Sixty percent of "second" marriages and seventy percent of "third" marriages will end in divorce court. Sixty-three percent of all families are headed by single parents. Eighty percent of all children will end up living in a single parent home. Fathers don't comply with child support orders, and mothers refuse to allow their children to see their fathers or paternal grandparents. Court dockets are bursting at the seams with divorce cases, motions to modify prior divorce decrees, child custody cases, cases involving spousal abuse and requests for child and spousal protection. Grandparents are getting into the act as state legislatures enact legislation giving them visitation rights with their grandchildren.

When I was growing up, divorce was the exception. Now divorce is the rule. Saying that divorce is an epidemic is an understatement. Divorce statistics only keep track of the relationships that fail following marriage ceremonies. These statistics do not reflect the millions of relationships that end each year outside the bounds of matrimony nor do they include all the people who choose to stay in unhappy marriages or unhealthy non-marital relationships. If you stop to think about it, it is unbelievable how little we know about creating healthy marriages and loving relationships.

From the first grade on, we learn how to read, write, do math, study history, etc. What we don't learn is how in this world to get along with one another, especially in marriage relationships.

SAD MEN/MAD WOMEN

I recently saw a deodorant commercial that had as its punch line "don't let 'em see you sweat." The message behind the ad illustrates how we, as a society, have learned how to hide what is actually going on inside ourselves. We value looking good more than being truthful and authentic. We have been trained to hide how we truly feel. This training in "hiding how we feel" has led us down a rose-colored path of attempting to look good on the outside while we have been dying spiritually and emotionally on the inside. We have been putting on a "looking good" act for so long we have lost the ability to identify or express how we truly feel. It shouldn't be much of a surprise that we find it difficult living with each other when we are alienated from our own emotional nature.

As a result of not being able to identify and express feelings, men and women have not fully developed emotionally or spiritually. As a direct result of our stunted emotional and spiritual growth, we lack the ability to form intimate and loving relationships and marriages.

Women have been coerced from early childhood not to feel or express anger. While women are being taught not to feel or express anger, males are being molded into "good little boys" and later into "real men" by a society that prohibits them from expressing sadness or acknowledging weakness and vulnerability. While both men and women have been coached not to cry, men are more likely not to express grief and sadness. By branding into our psyche the male script of "rough, tough and hard to bluff" and the female script of "nice and never angry," our culture has emotionally crippled both men and women. As a result of our male/female identity conditioning, marriages are made up of sad-acting women who are so angry they can't see straight and angry-acting men who are desperately sad. As long as women do not allow themselves to feel and express anger and men try to emulate the emotional sterility of Rambo or Dirty Harry, we will continue to suffer the pain of loneliness, imbalance, and pretense and assuredly fail at all attempts at happiness and intimacy. Until we learn how to identify and express all our emotions, we

3

will continue to be emotionally lopsided and unskilled at creating and sustaining healthy relationships.

When the outside doesn't match the inside, not only are you dishonest with yourself, but you invite emotional pain and relationship failure in your life.

NUMBING OUT

Our generation has inherited a bias against experiencing pain. Physical pain relievers are so common that suffering even from the slight pain of a headache is rarely tolerated. Psychiatrists hand out mood-altering chemicals to their clients like people hand out candy to neighborhood trick-or-treaters. Spiritual and emotional pain does not disappear under these circumstances but is masked and hidden behind a quick fix. Usually the pain is a symptom of an unhealthy lifestyle pattern. Drugs do not treat the lifestyle pattern but bring the instant relief we have become accustomed to according to our desire to live pain free.

It should not be surprising that there are so many children experimenting with and getting hooked on drugs. Our children are acting out adult behaviors and lifestyles they witnessed while they were growing up. Today's children are attempting to cope with the pressures, requirements, disappointments and joys of life with alcohol, pot, cocaine and crack. This drug use copies their parents' use of alcohol, tobacco, caffeine, Librium and

Valium. It's the same song their parents sang with a few new lyrics. The message children have grown up with is "if you are uncomfortable or in pain, you need to take some type of chemical to relieve the symptoms." Our children have learned well -- they have had excellent teachers.

Kids won't necessarily do what their parents tell them to do...

But they will always do what their parents do.

SHUT THAT KID UP

Watch what happens the next time you observe a child crying in public. First, the parents will get embarrassed and attempt to end the crying as quickly as possible. If the crying persists, other adults will become uncomfortable because their own emotional pain is activated by the baby's tears.

As adults we have successfully "shut up" (shut down) our own inner emotional life. The paradox is that by attempting to avoid experiencing pain, or hiding our pain, we prolong the pain and enhance its impact. A friend of mine used to say that hiding our pain was like trying to hold beach balls under water -- it robs you of your energy, and the beach balls will eventually surface.

We who have experienced the challenge of divorce have been poorly equipped to communicate effectively within a marriage relationship. We have been encouraged and trained to hide and cover up our feelings by denying that we are experiencing them or to drug them out of existence. We have covered up, hidden, denied, and drugged our emotional identities so successfully that we have left ourselves emotionally impotent and unable to form loving relationships. The number of divorces and the lack of intimacy in

8

our culture illustrate in an observable way the lack of emotional and spiritual development in our culture.

Hiding or burying our feelings and emotions is unhealthy and will result in relationship problems.

MY FIRST DIVORCE CLIENT

I began practicing law in 1974. Right off the bat, I started representing clients who were dealing with the calamity of divorce. My first divorce client was an attractive woman in her mid-twenties who had married a real sick man. The second day into their honeymoon, her husband started beating her up. She was hospitalized twice from his beatings, and she reported that besides being physically abused, her husband emotionally harassed her day and night at home and on her job.

It was a real pleasure for me to help this client who was a true "damsel in distress." She followed my advice, went to divorce court, was extracted out of a sick marriage, got her maiden name back and received a good share of the marital property. I felt like the Lone Ranger who had saved the day without the aid of Tonto.

I had patted myself on the back too soon. My self-adulation came to a screeching halt nine months later when this same client came back for additional help. She had married another wife beater. My client appeared even more distressed than before. My balloon popped. My education in law school had not prepared me to deal effectively with the emotional and spiritual needs of divorce clients. It became clear to me that helping divorce clients through the legal hoops did not ensure that they would not end up in other unsuccessful relationships and marriages. No one in law school had even discussed how to help people avoid "re-cycling" themselves over and over again in unworkable and painful relationships. I began to see that the court system not only lacked emotional sensitivity to families in the throes of divorce but actually encouraged conflict between divorcing spouses which led to more heartache and suffering. The legal system, as it applies to divorce cases, resembles a boxing match where clients and their lawyers slug it out over money, property and child custody -- not a pretty sight.

No one wins in divorce court.

BACK TO SCHOOL

After witnessing the emotional pain and turmoil that accompanied every divorce case and feeling helpless in the midst of so much human suffering (especially during repeat performances), I decided to go back to school and study psychology and counseling. In 1978, I enrolled in a guidance and counseling graduate program at a local university. In 1980, I moved to Hawaii and entered a graduate program in psychology and marriage and family therapy. During the two years I went to school and lived in Honolulu, I worked as a clinical director of an alcohol and drug rehabilitation center, provided marriage and family therapy services for a local church and practiced law on a part-time basis. After I moved back to Missouri, I attended and graduated from a two-year seminary program and became an ordained minister. During seminary and the time spent in graduate schools, I continued practicing family law.

Today I spend most of my lawyering time involved in divorce and custody litigation. Most of my counseling time is taken up doing marriage, addiction, and co-dependency counseling. I spend most of my ministering time presenting classes, seminars and workshops on relationships and emotional and spiritual healing. In my spare time, I do divorce mediation. I hope mediation will become a more preferred method of handling divorce cases in the future as compared with the traditional "knock down - drag out" divorce litigation process that most people presently endure.

My educational pursuits after law school have helped me understand and empathize more with people who embrace the divorce experience. This education has also helped me heal from several personal relationship failures, including my own divorce. I believe that if you do not learn how to relate differently to yourself and others, you will continue to repeat the past. A buddy of mine says it this way: "If you keep on doin' what you've always done, you'll keep on gettin' what you've always gotten." If you do not develop new relationship skills, you will end up building new relationships based upon a set of old relationship blueprints that didn't work in the first place.

This book will help you draft a new set of blueprints -- ones that are free of chronic fears, resentments, feelings of guilt and self-defeating behavior. If you have the desire to do "whatever it takes" to rehabilitate your emotional and spiritual consciousness and you are willing to follow the suggestions contained in this book, I predict you will experience more joy and happiness than you ever believed possible.

II. WHO IS RESPONSIBLE FOR THE SHAPE I'M IN?

Adam blamed Eve, Eve blamed the snake and the beat goes on. (2)

HELEN AND BEN

Helen and Ben arrived at my office one day for marriage counseling. When I asked them about the nature of their problem, Helen replied: "I'm upset because Ben's upset that I'm upset because. . ." Ben told me, "I'm upset because she's upset because. . ." I asked them if they would be willing to play a game called "Taking Responsibility For Your Own Stuff," and they said they would give it a try. I again asked Helen to explain any problems or struggles she was having, and the following dialogue took place:

Helen: "I'm upset because he's. . ."

Me: "Helen, excuse me for interrupting you, but this is how the "Taking Responsibility For Your Own Stuff Game" works. You have to be responsible for what is going on with you, which means that you can't make your husband responsible for what you are emotionally experiencing. Do you understand?"

Helen: "Yes."

Me: "Please explain why you are here today."

Helen: "I'm upset!"

Me: "There is a great deal we can do to help you not be upset if not being upset is your goal. As long as the reason you are upset is due to what your husband does or doesn't do or is attributable to his attitudes or his feelings, then I'm afraid there isn't much we can do, because your emotional stability or lack of stability will be dependent upon what's going on with him."

Helen kind of shook her head, looked at me funny and said, "You mean it's that simple?"

I told her that the work she would need to do in order to become less upset and depressed wouldn't be easy, but taking responsibility for her own emotional health was that simple.

17

It is incredible how many people are walking around feeling upset because someone else has chosen to be upset. A lot of people believe that they are responsible for other people's feelings, other people's lives, other people's happiness. If you are wired to believe that you are responsible for another person's happiness and that person isn't doing well, then isn't it your fault? If you believe the underlying premise that you are responsible for someone else, then yes, it is your fault because it is your responsibility to see to it that the other person is okay. But guess what? No person is responsible for another person's happiness, life or emotional security. That means that you are not responsible for anyone else's happiness, and it also means that no one is responsible for your happiness. Well, you say, what happened to the "I am going to make them happy so they will make me happy" story line? You can see the logical conclusion of that story line everyday in divorce court -- the story line is a vicious lie. The mistaken belief that anyone has the power, or even has the right, to be responsible for someone else's life, security or happiness will always ensure relationship failure.

Who is responsible for the shape you are in? **You are!** I'm sure that there have been many bad things that happened to you in the past, over which you had little or no control. Maybe you have some really good reasons to stay mad at someone or sad about something that happened. We all could write out a long list of excellent reasons to stay mad and sad over how life has worked out up until now. The people and experiences that have caused us pain may have been responsible for how we felt at the time we were hurt or injured. However, YOU are the only person who can take responsibility for the way your life is going to be from this moment on. If you are still allowing a past injury to re-cycle around and around in your heart and head, that is your choice.

Recovering from divorce requires that you heal from the hurts, fears, resentments and feelings of guilt that you have accumulated during your lifetime, including the emotional wounds you experienced during your marriage. Section V of this book on emotional and spiritual healing will give you the tools to heal the wounds from your past. In order to begin the healing process it is imperative that you assert to yourself that you are the responsible party for your own recovery and for your own life.

The root of most relationship problems is the unrealistic belief and expectation that the other person in the relationship is responsible for the way it is (for you) or the way it is going to be (for you). A common complaint that divorce clients verbalize is that their spouses didn't make them happy. These clients have been waiting for their mates to figure out how to make them happy. The key to solving relationship problems is the belief and expectation that you are responsible for the way it is (for you) and the way it is going to be (for you).

God will give you all the strength, guidance and wisdom needed in order for you to heal and live a happy, joyous and success "full" life. However, you must do the footwork. The footwork begins with your taking responsibility for your own stuff. Your own stuff consists of your own feelings (not theirs), your own life (not theirs), your physical, emotional and spiritual health and well-being (not theirs) and your own experiences in life (not theirs). In our culture both men and women are deluded into thinking that they are responsible for other people's stuff. While we stay busy trying to make others happy, we do not take the time to develop the capacity to meet our own needs. The recovery process outlined in this book involves healing the emotional wounds of the past and learning how to meet OUR OWN emotional and spiritual needs. As you read on, you will not be encouraged to find the right person "out there" somewhere. You will be encouraged to become a whole, healthy and spiritually guided individual who has developed the capacities to love and accept love. Taking responsibility for your own life is the first step in becoming receptive to the possibility of healing and learning how to become a healthy participant in a loving relationship.

THE FOUR FUNCTIONS OF CONSCIOUSNESS

In order to emotionally heal, it is necessary to understand and make peace with your own inner world. The diagram below illustrates four functions of consciousness that make up your inner world. Your sense of reality and your ability to function in the world and in relationships are determined by your thoughts, feelings, physical sensations and Spirit.

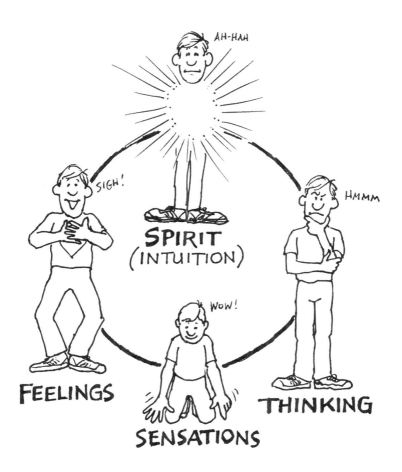

Emotional healing, successful living and loving relationships result from living life according to spiritual principles that are discerned through our intuitive connection with Spirit. Spirit is our direct channel to the wisdom and healing power of God. Intuition is the ear through which we hear the *"still small voice"* of Spirit. (3) Intuition is the pathway to spiritual healing, guidance and inspiration. Truth with a capital "T" is available to each one of us through our intuitive link with our own spiritual nature.

The *"Kingdom of God"* is accessible through our spiritual function of consciousness. (4) The problem is that we are distracted by and obsessed with the other levels of consciousness. Our distractions and obsessions with feelings, thoughts and sensations block off our access to our intuitive connection with the sunlight of Spirit.

This is why it is difficult to spiritually awaken.

ADDICTIONS

We live in an age of addictions. People who are addicted to or obsessed with one thing or another usually feel empty and lonely. They feel fractional and not whole. People go through life looking for people, substances, places and events to make them feel full and complete. This search always goes unfulfilled (unfilled) and leads to chronic unhappiness and frustration. The unhappiness and frustration are temporarily avoided by more or new addictive behaviors and substances. The common denominator in all addictive behaviors is a focus upon experiences and substances outside oneself. Addicts are alienated and emotionally detached from their own inner world of Spirit.

During a divorce, spouses will tend to obsess and fixate on outer substances, objects and activities -- outside the realm of intuition and Spirit. The following is a partial list of addictive activities, objects and substances:

food;
caffeine;
sex;
alcohol;
other mind-altering chemicals;
work;
relationships;
television;
gambling;
books;
sugar;
physical abuse;
shopping;
worrying;
feeling guilty; and
feeling fearful and resentful.

The key in determining whether or not you are addicted to anything on the list, or something else, is to ask yourself if the substance, object or behavior is causing problems. If it is causing you problems, then you have a problem with it. If drinking alcohol causes problems, then you have a drinking problem. If gambling is causing problems, you have a gambling problem. If worrying is causing problems, you have a worrying problem. These activities are addictions if you can't stop doing them. If you continue doing something that causes problems -- you are addicted.

During a divorce, many people become involved in addictive thinking, feeling or behavior. If an addiction was present prior to the divorce, the divorce process intensifies the addictive condition. If you are addicted to or fixated upon someone or something, you have already found out that there isn't much time in your day to devote to spiritual pursuits or emotional healing.

FEELING--THINKING TUG OF WAR

Most people, especially those involved in a divorce, are stuck in a feeling--thinking tug of war. They wake up in the morning with a thought that provokes a feeling, which reminds them of another thought, that initiates another feeling, which ignites another thought. This rambling back and forth between our thoughts and feelings reminds me of the story of the man, who was walking down the street, minding his own business. All of a sudden, out of nowhere the man was attacked -- by his own mind. Like the man who was attacked by his own mind, we all are held hostage by the never-ending dialogue between our thoughts and feelings that constantly compete for our attention. Our thoughts and feelings "carry on" like two three-year-olds who want the same piece of candy. We are unable to seek ". . .*first the kingdom of God*. . ." due to the powerful distractive influence of our thinking and feeling processes. (5) The intensity of this feeling-thinking tug of war escalates during the time of divorce.

THE DANCE OF FEAR

The leading cause of marital demise is the dance of fear. The steps and tempo of the dance are orchestrated and motivated by fear. The fear in question usually does not surface until one of the spouses begins to lose some of the strong romantic feelings he or she experienced early in the relationship. It is just a matter of time until the intensity of the romantic stage of the relationship begins to subside. When the intensity begins to dissipate, the spouses must then deal with the fears they both have that lurk just below the surface of the romantic stage.

There are two distinct fears that make up the dance, and they both operate on different ends of the same pendulum. One of these fears is the fear of abandonment. The other fear is the fear of engulfment. We all have these fears, and the fears themselves do not destroy relationships. However, misinterpreting these fears may spell doom for a relationship especially if each spouse blames the other spouse for the fear he or she experiences. The fear and discomfort felt by a spouse during the dance is caused by his or her own emotional makeup and not by something that the other spouse is doing or has done.

The dance begins when Tarzan meets Jane.

Jane is absolutely wonderful according to Tarzan. She is everything he has ever wanted and although his last relationship ended in divorce, he knows for sure that Jane is different; she is definitely the one for him. Jane realizes that Tarzan is the catch of a lifetime. Tarzan represents everything Jane has ever wanted in a relationship, rolled up in one man. There is electricity in the air and intense hormonal activity coursing through their veins.

The romantic stage will last as long as it does. During the romantic stage, Jane and Tarzan remain emotionally and physically close to each other -- they both feel secure and happy. Life couldn't be any better. Tarzan and Jane decide to get married. The wedding is a success, and it looks like "happily ever after" is going to be a reality.

Let's look in on Tarzan and Jane one year later. We find that the romantic edge is wearing a little thin for Tarzan. We find that Jane is just as strongly "in (romantic) love" as she was when she first fell in love with Tarzan. Tarzan, on the other hand, is not quite as "in (romantic) love" with Jane. Tarzan's hormone production has slowed down considerably, and he begins to feel trapped and engulfed. Tarzan feels suffocated and threatened by Jane's constant closeness. Tarzan starts to back off from Jane emotionally and physically. While avoiding Jane he tells her, "I just need a little space," or "I've got to have a little breathing room."

Tarzan is suffering from his own fears of engulfment. These engulfment fears have been inside Tarzan since childhood but up until now were masked and outranked by the intensity of the romantic stage. Jane, meanwhile, will interpret this change in Tarzan's attitude and behavior as the beginning of the end of a wonderful relationship. Jane will counter Tarzan's retreating behavior with her attempts at getting closer to Tarzan, fueled by her fear of abandonment. Jane will experience feelings of rejection, feelings of loss, feelings of being left behind and all alone. Jane, out of her fear of abandonment, will pursue Tarzan with vigor.

Jane's fear of abandonment has been part of her emotional makeup since her early childhood. The intensity of the romantic stage masked and outranked her fear of abandonment until Tarzan needed "a little space," which was caused by his fear of engulfment. As Jane continues her pursuit, Tarzan will feel more trapped and smothered (engulfed) and will feel the need to escape from Jane. Jane, in turn, will try to get closer, and "around and around they will dance" to the rhythm of their fears.

Finally, Jane will get tired of pursuing Tarzan. By this time Jane will feel hurt, betrayed, angry and convinced that Tarzan is a jerk. At this point in time, it is clear to Jane that her pain resulted from Tarzan's lack of commitment, unpredictability and dishonesty. Tarzan is convinced that his pain was caused by Jane's demandingness, clinging behavior and insecurity. Neither Jane nor Tarzan realizes that the discomfort and pain are caused by her or his own fears of abandonment and engulfment.

Disgusted and upset with Tarzan, Jane will eventually begin to move away from Tarzan. Tarzan will see that Jane is no longer trying to pursue him, and he will relax and feel relieved -- for a while.

When Jane moves a little further away, Tarzan will start to panic as his fear of abandonment is activated. Feeling rejected, and fearing the loss of Jane, Tarzan will pursue her and apologize for being such an uncaring jerk. He will attempt to explain to Jane that there has been a misunderstanding, and now that he has had "his space" he is sure that everything will be great, just like the way it used to be.

Tarzan will tell Jane anything she needs to hear in order to convince her to "come back" to him. After Jane allows Tarzan back into her good graces (and she will), they will be close again, and life will be rosy -- (for a while) --

until the renewed closeness triggers Tarzan's or Jane's engulfment fears.

The dance of fear continues although each partner will take turns in leading and following -- retreating and chasing -- pursuing and avoiding. Does this look familiar? I'll bet it does. This dance will drive fifty to seventy percent of all married couples into divorce court. Spouses who do not divorce will strike an unconscious bargain with the other spouse whereby they will stay far enough away from one another so their fears of engulfment won't kick in and stay close enough to the other so that their fears of abandonment won't be awakened -- a safe non-intimate relationship.

Many people find themselves "stuck" between the fear of intimacy and the fear of abandonment.

These relationships remind me of the baby bear's porridge in "Goldilocks and the Three Bears" -- not too hot (not too close or intimate), not too cold (not too far away) but just right (no fear of abandonment or engulfment). The problem with a safe non-intimate relationship is that the people in them still need passion and intimacy in their lives. People who find themselves in safe non-intimate relationships will either die a slow emotional death or seek passion and intimacy outside the relationship, which will create more heartache and suffering and eventually lead to divorce court.

III. WHAT TO DO FOR SHORT TERM RELIEF

When in doubt -- pray.

PRAY AND KEEP ON PRAYING

I grew up near the buckle of the "Bible Belt." When I was a little boy, I heard a lot about a God that sounded like he was going to get me. It seemed to me that this God's main purpose was to keep score on all the bad stuff I did and then one day zap me from on high. My imagination pictured this God, having long white hair, including a beard and mustache. The most frightening part of the picture was God's frowning and angry face.

The imagined God of my childhood was angry and terrifying.

Since my early childhood, I have learned about another God. I have found help, peace and comfort in the God of my adult understanding who is loving, nurturing, kind, generous, gentle, forgiving and who has a great sense of humor. I now believe that life is not about feeling guilty or about fearing God based on the false notion that God is going to hurt us. Life is about receiving and giving love, compassion, understanding and forgiveness. Prayer always works, and prayer always works during a divorce. God's grace is inexhaustible and always available.

Most people have learned, or at least have heard, that our extremity is God's opportunity. However, during times that we desperately need God's help, many of us often forget to ask for it. There is no outer experience, including divorce, that is greater or stronger than God within you. ". . .*he who is in you is greater than he who is in the world.*" *(6)* No matter how bad your life looks, and it may look extremely shabby going through a divorce, God's presence, peace and healing love are with you always. It may be impossible to feel good during your divorce as you experience your share of hurt and pain. The grief, sadness and depression you will encounter are appropriate emotional responses to the loss of your marriage.

Major changes begin to take place during a divorce. You will face the death of a dream, the death of a relationship and a change in relationships with friends and family members. You will experience a change in your identity, a change in your family's identity and emotional changes in you and your children. People who divorce are in crisis. The crisis can be an opportunity to heal emotionally and evolve spiritually. Keeping your eye on God and knowing that God's "everlasting arms" are an ever present comfort will help you "hang in there."

During those times, you harass yourself with all the "whys," all the "coulda-shoulda-woulda's," and all the "if only's"; remember to "*Trust in the Lord with all thine heart and lean not unto thine own understanding.*" *(7)* Trusting, including trusting in God, is no easy task during a divorce. However, if you can muster even the smallest amount of trust and faith in God, the door to God's guidance, wisdom and healing power will open to you.

41

Ask, seek and knock. *"Seek ye first the kingdom of God. . ."* and all things will work out in divine order. (8)

Many things will happen during your divorce that will not make any sense nor seem fair. Each day make a conscious decision to turn your life, divorce case, spouse, children, family, lawyer and legal system over to God's care. In prayer, "let go and let God."

Follow the *"still small voice"* within you, regarding how to pray. (9) If you are finding yourself unable to form a prayer request concerning your divorce, consider using the following prayer:

> *God, this sure is a hard time for me and all those who are affected by this divorce experience. I pray that you touch my heart and the hearts of everyone else who suffers over the ending of this relationship. Remind us that your healing currents of love constantly flow through each of us like a powerful river. Thank you for the abundance of courage, peace, guidance, love and compassion that you have placed within our souls. Let me remember to keep you on my mind and in my heart as I lean on you and trust in your grace and goodness. Thank you God. Amen.*

If you can't remember this prayer, use the short version -- "help." Practice experiencing the presence of God. Wherever you go, God goes with you. Whatever happens, God's healing love is available to you. You will find that prayer will give you the strength, courage and wisdom to "make it" one day at a time.

Throughout the day, pause often and focus your attention on God. Concentrate on your breathing, and as you breathe, imagine breathing in the healing spirit of God. If you find yourself irritated or worried about someone or something, visualize with your imagination God's love surrounding and healing that person or situation. Feel God's love bringing peace and harmony into your heart. When in doubt, when angry, when depressed, when fearful, when feeling guilty, become still and fill your mind with thoughts of God. *"Be still, and know that I am God. . ." (10)*

A prayer which holds a special place in my heart is the Serenity Prayer:

"God grant me the serenity to accept the things I cannot change, the courage to change the things I can and the wisdom to know the difference." (11)

The Serenity Prayer is an excellent resource upon which to focus, especially in times of fear and turmoil. It will help you apply the Serenity Prayer to your life if you keep in mind that you do not have the power to change anyone but yourself.

FIND EMOTIONAL SUPPORT AND NOT FROM YOUR FAMILY

Before I agree to represent divorce clients, as an attorney, I make sure that they are receiving emotional support or that they agree to reach out for emotional help. I ordinarily will not accept a divorce case unless the client is in counseling or agrees to participate in counseling. I also believe that one's own family is usually the worst place to search for emotional help during the crisis of a divorce. I have seen families turn into the Hatfields and McCoys more times than I would like to remember.

Seeking advice and support from family members can make matters worse. Instead of sharing and reducing your pain, confiding in relatives may intensify your pain and magnify the conflict between yourself and your spouse. Getting your clan to agree with you that "he is a no good s.o.b.," or that "she was always a little troublemaker" will not benefit you or your family. Recruiting a "he or she is to blame" cheerleading squad might give you a temporary sense of satisfaction. However, getting your family to side with you (and against him or her) will end up hurting you, your children and your family. As a general rule, leave your family out of your divorce as much as possible. Families are usually too emotionally involved to give objective support to a family member who is going through a divorce. Seeking comfort from your side of the family may lead to more tension and conflict for all concerned.

A counselor's office and support groups are healthy places to find emotional support.

GET INTO COUNSELING

Finding a healthy counselor who can help you work through your emotional pain needs to be a top priority. The time is ripe to grieve over and emotionally heal from the death of your marriage. It is also an exceptional time to work through and heal childhood and adolescent emotional issues that in all likelihood helped cause the demise of your marriage. If you don't deal with your emotional pain, you will find yourself involved in another relationship just like the last one (or worse). If you don't resolve the emotional conflict of your past, including the wounds of your latest failed attempt at marriage, you will never escape the pain of your past and remain forever tied to it like a tree to its roots. You have to change in order for your relationships to change. You have to get healthier in order for your relationships to get healthier. If you do not get emotional help at this critical stage in your life, you will find yourself getting involved in another unsuccessful relationship, and another, and another etc. Getting into counseling may help you avoid the following three act play:

ACT ONE   love, romance and marriage;

ACT TWO   fault-finding in your spouse, the inability to be intimate due to your own insecurity and defensiveness that you don't see in yourself but you see clearly in him or her; and

ACT THREE   another painful separation and another trip to your lawyer's office.

Make a commitment to your health and well-being right now. If you are going through a divorce, seek counseling. If you are divorced and haven't gone through counseling, either seek counseling now or at least go to counseling during your next relationship merry-go-round, which probably will be happening sometime soon.

Going to a counselor can be scary. Who wants to tell some stranger all the intimate details of your life, especially all the embarrassing stuff -- you remember -- the stuff you told yourself you would never tell anyone? Going to counseling is risky business. There are some pretty crazy people who are attempting to save the world with their therapy skills while at the same time remaining tied up in emotional knots themselves. Beware especially of spiritual or religious counselors who do not understand or find value in psychology and psychology-oriented counselors who do not understand or value spiritual healing and recovery. A good counselor is worth his or her weight in gold. A bad counselor can do real damage to you. Good counselors do exist, and the following guide-lines will help you find a good one.

During your search for a good counselor, pray for guidance. Ask your friends about their experiences with counselors. Be sure to interview several counselors. Set up a 30-minute session with each counselor that you interview. Ask in advance how much half an hour of his or her time will cost. During the session, tell the counselor that you are looking for someone who can help you through the emotional stress of a divorce. Also take a friend with you to these interviews. Ask the counselors you interview the following questions:

1. Have you ever been divorced? If the counselor has been divorced, ask how many times? What did you do to work through the emotional impact you ex-perienced? When were you divorced? You don't want to be in therapy with someone who is in the middle of his or her own divorce or recently divorced.
2. Are you married, and if so, when were you married?
3. What did you do before you became a counselor, and why did you become a counselor?
4. How many sessions do you believe it will take to complete the therapy process?
5. Do you believe in divorce, and what are your thoughts and beliefs about divorce?
6. What is your religious and spiritual background, and what are your religious and spiritual beliefs as they pertain to counseling?
7. Who do I remind you of?

8. Do you enjoy divorce counseling?
9. What other information do you have that might help me decide whether or not to become your client?
10. What other counselors would you recommend?
11. What do you enjoy the most about counseling?
12. What do you enjoy the least about counseling?
13. What is your educational background, and what are your counseling credentials?"
14. What support groups would you recommend in our community?
15. What books on divorce would you recommend?

The counselors' responses to these questions should give you some important information upon which to base your choice.

After each interview, pray for guidance and discuss the interview with the friend who accompanied you to the interview. As a general rule, it's better to choose a female counselor if you are female and a male counselor if you are male. Find the counselor that intuitively feels right to you. Take your time and shop around. Also ask each counselor you interview what attorneys she or he would recommend to represent you in your divorce case. After you choose a counselor, you can always choose again if the first one doesn't work out to your satisfaction. In any event, get into counseling with someone you feel good about and find a support group that can help you meet your emotional and spiritual needs.

If your life has been adversely affected by a friend's or relative's drinking, I would recommend that you attend Alanon meetings. (12) Many of my divorce and counseling clients have received immense help from participating in Alanon. Alanon probably will be listed in your phone book. If not, contact Alcoholics Anonymous and ask if they can help you locate an Alanon meeting. (13)

1.   QUIT FIGHTING. Quit fighting with the other parent. It is difficult to set aside your emotional desire to "get even" with or strike back at someone with whom you identify so much pain. You might say that you can't stop the conflict because he or she always argues with you, and you can't control him or her. However, it still takes "two to tango" and two to fight. Although you can't control what the other parent does, you can control your own mouth and your own behavior -- with practice.

Children are at risk of being damaged before, during and after a divorce by their parents' conflict. Substantial emotional scarring is sustained by children when their parents continue to fight. It is important for you to experience your feelings and do whatever is necessary to ventilate and express your emotions. However, do your ventilating in your counselor's office and not around your children or soon to be ex-spouse. Verbal attacks and snide remarks aimed at the other parent have the effect of tearing away pieces of your children's souls. The more you fight with the other parent, the more you ensure that your children will receive emotional wounds that may never heal.

STOP IT!

52

2.   Encourage your child to love the other parent. The other parent represents a critically important and necessary part of your child's life. Encouraging your child to love the other parent will have the effect of helping your child love himself or herself. If you, through your actions, "put down" the other parent, your behavior will have the effect of chipping away at your child's self-esteem and identity. Remember, you can kick, scream, cuss, ridicule and explode in your counselor's office. The ventilating you do with your counselor will emotionally benefit you, and it won't hurt your children. Keep the emotional conflict away from your children, and do your best to encourage love for your former spouse.   Your children are not divorcing the other parent.

Your attitude toward the other parent will have a lasting effect on your children.

3.   Explain, more than once, to your children that they did not cause the divorce. Your children will tend to blame themselves for the divorce. Young children often believe that if they would have acted better, Mommy and Daddy wouldn't have separated. Spend time explaining to your children that the divorce was not caused by anything your children did or didn't do.

4.   Allow your children to have their own feelings and their own experiences. There is a certain satisfaction that parents feel when their children experience the same feelings they do, especially during divorce. Parents are comforted by the belief that their child perceives life the same way they do.   Mommy appreciates that "her" son Joey is mad at Daddy too. Daddy feels reassured when Joey tells him that, "Mommy has been mean to Daddy." In an effort to please each parent, children will deny their own feelings and take on those of their parents. When Joey is with Mommy, he is mad at Daddy and when he visits Daddy, he is mad at Mommy. By allowing your child to have his or her own feelings and experiences, you will positively promote your child's emotional health and development.

Your children will experience a wide range of emotions. Allow them to have their own emotions, and do not look to your children for your emotional support. Look to your counselor, friends and support groups for your support. Your child is not equipped to be your therapist. Whatever you do, do not ask or encourage your child to choose sides. Also talk about your children with your counselor. Your counselor can help you determine if your children need professional help.

5.   Take care of yourself. Get plenty of rest, good food and exercise. You will help your children by staying healthy and modeling sane behaviors. You will hurt your children by staying sick and modeling insane behaviors.

6.   There are many good books that have been written on divorce and the impact divorce has upon children and the family. The bibliography on page 111 and 112 lists several books you may find helpful.

.

FIND A SANE, COMPETENT AND CARING ATTORNEY

QUESTION: What is black and brown and looks good on a divorce attorney?

ANSWER: A doberman.

QUESTION: What do you have when there are 1,000 divorce attorneys on the bottom of the ocean?

ANSWER: A good start.

Divorce attorneys are not the most loved players in drama of divorce. Most people dislike the idea of going to an attorney for any reason. No one likes spending money in exchange for legal advice about his or her divorce. Also, talking to an attorney about the details of the relationship you had with your spouse is awkward and embarrassing.

Some people complain about the experiences they have had with their divorce attorneys. Their attorneys wouldn't return their phone calls or sold them down the river. Their attorneys didn't explain anything to them or just took their money and didn't do anything. Their attorneys weren't empathetic or didn't bring out enough in court or were in cahoots with the other attorney, etc. There is no doubt that some clients have legitimate complaints. However, if you carefully interview prospective lawyers, many potential difficulties and communication problems can be avoided. Like counselors or other professionals, there are competent attorneys and incompetent attorneys. If you work at it, you will find the right attorney for you. You want to find and retain a sane, competent and caring attorney with whom you feel comfortable and confident.

The following suggestions will help you with your selection of any attorney. Set up a 30-minute session with each attorney that you intend to interview. Find out in advance how much the half hour will cost. Try to talk to each attorney at the time you make your appointments. Take a friend with you to your appointments. Ask each attorney that you interview the following questions:

1. Have you ever been divorced, and if so, how many times? What did you do in order to work through the emotional impact you experienced?
2. How much will this divorce cost, how much is your retainer fee, and will there be any other fees or costs?
3. Do you enjoy practicing divorce law, and if so, why? If the answer is no, thank the attorney for his or her time and <u>exit</u>.
4. What other lawyers would you recommend in this area of law, what counselors would you recommend, and why?
5. Will you promptly return my phone calls?
6. Will anyone else in your office be working on my case? If there will be others, ask who and why?
7. What do you enjoy the most about practicing law?
8. What do you enjoy the most about practicing divorce law?
9. What do you enjoy the least about practicing law?
10. What do you enjoy the least about practicing divorce law?
11. May I call you at your home and is your home telephone number listed in the telephone book? If the phone number is not listed, ask why?
12. Do you specialize in divorce work?
13. What other information do you have that might help me decide whether or not to become your client?

Interview several prospective attorneys. Pray for guidance after each interview, and discuss the interviews with the friend who accompanies you. Also remember you can fire an attorney and hire another one if your first choice doesn't work out.

IF POSSIBLE, MEDIATE YOUR DIVORCE

"Blessed are the peacemakers. . ." (14)

Back in 1975 or thereabouts, there was a circuit judge in Springfield, Missouri, named Jack Powell. I had known Judge Powell since childhood and had always known him to have a kind and caring spirit. I served on a divorce mediation committee with Judge Powell when divorce mediation was virtually unheard of in our neck of the woods. I will always remember how committed Judge Powell was in finding alternative ways for resolving domestic disputes. He recognized that during a divorce, the legal process assessed a tragic toll upon families. He was particularly sensitive to the impact of divorce upon children. Judge Powell died before mediation caught on in our community. Judge Powell knew long ago, as I do now, that divorce mediation is a positive alternative to the adversarial system that resembles an emotional war zone where families and children are injured.

Everyone gets hurt in a court fight.

Most people turn their divorce cases over to three strangers -- two attorneys and a judge. Then these three strangers end up making critical decisions about their lives, their children and their property. The decisions made by these three people will affect everyone in the family for the rest of their lives. Mediation allows and encourages spouses to take responsibility for their own divorce agreement. Spouses themselves decide all the important issues, such as child custody arrangements and child support; property and debt distribution; spousal support and who pays court costs, attorney fees and mediation expenses. The mediation process as compared with the traditional divorce process in Missouri:

1. Is private not public;
2. Is cooperative not adversarial;
3. Usually takes 60 to 90 days as compared with eight months to two years;
4. Provides opportunities to emotionally heal and reconcile differences instead of fostering more hurt, rigidity and suffering;
5. Involves less conflict;
6. Usually costs less; and
7. Leads to fewer trips back into court after the divorce is over.

Mediation, which is based upon cooperation and openness, is a rational alternative to the traditional legal system which is inherently adversarial.

See Appendixes B, C, and D on pages 113 through 124 for additional information on mediation.

ACTIVELY PARTICIPATE IN YOUR DIVORCE -- STUDY THE LAW

I encourage you to actively participate in your divorce case. If you mediate your divorce, you will automatically take an active role as a result of the way mediation works. Even if you are unable to mediate your dispute and you rely entirely upon the court system and your attorney, get involved in your divorce case. Learn as much as you can about the divorce laws in your state, under which your case will be negotiated or litigated.

Each state has its own divorce laws. These laws are based upon statutory law and case law that change from time to time. Appendix E on pages 125 through 142 contain statutory sections of Missouri divorce law cover the requirements for a divorce, property distribution, alimony, child support and child custody. These statutes may or may not be similar to the divorce statutes in your state. Ask your attorney to give you a copy of the statutes that apply to the issues in your divorce case. In Missouri, a divorce is called a dissolution of marriage, and alimony is called maintenance.

Studying the law is no substitute for hiring a good mediator and attorney. Your own study of the law will help you help yourself, your mediator and your attorney prepare your case to be successfully settled or litigated. Trying to represent yourself in a divorce case is like trying to do your own root canal work. Root canal work requires the skill of a good dentist. Divorce litigation requires the skills of good attorneys, and divorce negotiation requires the skills of good mediators and attorneys.

IV. EMOTIONAL AND SPIRITUAL HEALING

The following eight steps or strategies will help you heal emotionally and spiritually from the wounds and injuries you have sustained from your divorce and from life in general. By following these steps your feet will be firmly placed on the road to happiness, joy and freedom as you shed unwanted behavior and attitudes and grasp a new view of your world.

If you are serious about experiencing emotional and spiritual healing, you will need to identify and heal from those experiences in your past when you were hurt and injured emotionally. These injuries include the times you were frightened, emotionally or physically abused, embarrassed, physically hurt, angered, disappointed, punished, etc. Accumulated fear, anger and guilt experiences block your attempts at intimacy and happiness. This emotional baggage from the past resides inside you. These emotions (fear, anger and guilt) will continue showing up in all your relationships until you take the necessary healing steps to clean up (emotionally neutralize) your past experiences. This emotional cleansing process is not easy. However, this cleansing process is necessary if you want to participate in successful relationships, including the relationships you have with yourself and with God. A relationship with another person wherein the needs of both parties are met in a mutually supportive environment is impossible until you do your own inner healing work.

An unprocessed and unhealed emotional past guarantees a life filled with frustration, unfulfillment and disharmony with yourself and others. Until inner harmony is achieved, your chances of happiness are nil, in or out of relationships. Relationships with others will only magnify the pain concealed in your own heart which is trapped in the past.

THANK YOU, BERIT AND HARVEY

My belief in the necessity of healing the past began with my own experience. In 1972, I was hospitalized for acute depression. I had withdrawn from life to the point of not being able to talk. I sat around in a zombie-like stupor, and any attempt at communicating with the outside world was excruciatingly painful. Never in my life had I felt such fear and pain. I had emotionally shut down and closed the door to my outside world. The psychiatrist in charge of my case believed that I would never regain my verbal skills, and my overall prognosis was poor. I had managed to become a candidate for long-term treatment and hospitalization.

66

While undergoing treatment, I met a woman named Berit, and we became friends. After I left the treatment facility, Berit telephoned and told me of a weekend retreat in Kansas City, Missouri, involving Re-evaluation Counseling. (15) She said that the results of this type of counseling were impressive.

Tears are the rain that cleanse the soul.

It seemed that a fellow in Seattle, Washington, named Harvey Jackins had developed a therapy method that helped teach people how to grieve over (and through) the pain of the past. Part of Jackins' counseling theory was based upon the belief that by talking about and emotionally re-experiencing the past, you would be able to grieve through unresolved painful experiences. As a result of this grief work, you would break through chronic and rigid behavior, feeling and thinking patterns. Without this breakthrough grieving process, you would likely stay emotionally chained to the painful effects of your past.

My initial experience at the Kansas City weekend retreat was unbelievably therapeutic. The retreat environment felt safe and supportive. With Berit's and Harvey's help I opened up, cried for the first time in years and began a grieving process that was long overdue. During the grief work came the opportunity to emotionally and intellectually "re-evaluate" past hurtful experiences. I began to emotionally resolve large chunks of my past that had been the sources of much pain and suffering. The weekend proved to be a powerful healing experience and the beginning of a healing journey I continue to travel. My weekend with Berit, Harvey and the other co-counselors gave me a second chance at life, and for that I will be forever grateful.

THE EFFECTS OF THE PAST

As I later studied counseling and psychology, I came to believe that most emotional suffering and the inability to love and be loved, is due to our unhealed past. Instead of healing our pain as we go through life, most of us suppress hurtful experiences, hoping the painful effects will go away. Later on in life we emotionally re-experience those past hurts as they reappear in new contexts and in new relationships. For example, a woman who is physically abused by her father will have a tendency to become involved with men who will physically or emotionally abuse her. The unresolved pain from her past (abuse from her father) will resurface in other relationships. It's as though unresolved pain has a life and identity all its own. This pain attempts to get our attention by showing up again and again in situations that become emotional re-enactments of the past. A client of mine was on her fourth marriage to her fourth alcoholic husband before she realized that her marriages were re-enactments of the relationship she had with her alcoholic father. We all find ourselves attracted to people who have qualities that will help us explore our own healing needs.

I have counseled with many people whose parents were often physically absent during their childhood -- parents who did not actively participate in their children's lives. These children grew up feeling unworthy and alone. Throughout their adult lives they chose mates who didn't like spending time with them and who devalued them. These clients, in their marriages, would re-create the kind of relationships they had previously experienced with their parents when they were growing up. They were attracted to marriage and relationship partners who were unable to emotionally commit to a relationship and who had difficulty with intimacy and closeness. Their partners fit the parent-child model with which they were reared. Their sadness and feelings of hopelessness continued to increase until they figured out that their relationships were being unconsciously hand-picked by their own inner need to heal the childhood trauma and grief they experienced when they were left alone and emotionally ignored by their parents.

69

The following two stories and the other stories that appear throughout the book have been shared by former counseling clients. These stories portray how powerfully the past influences our identities and our relationship expectations and patterns.

BONNIE

I guess I have always been fearful to some extent. But when I began my divorce proceedings and filed for divorce, I couldn't believe the amount of fear that I felt. It was like I was surrounded by a black cloud of fear all of the time. I went into isolation. I was even uncomfortable around my best friends. I felt intimidated by the legal system, and I was afraid to open up with my counselor. All I really wanted to do was stay in bed and hide under the covers. This didn't make sense to me because I really and truly wanted out of my marriage. My ex-husband had put me down emotionally for over ten years and occasionally pushed and punched me around physically. I definitely wanted out -- finally! I guess I was afraid of the unknown. I knew what it was like putting up with my husband's constant criticism and occasional physical abuse, but I didn't know what it was going to be like when I was finally out of that mess.

I began learning in therapy that the treatment I had received from my husband was nothing new. I had always gotten involved in relationships with men who were judgmental, highly critical and physically abusive. I would always feel guilty when I was criticized regardless of whether or not the criticism was justified or not. The first man who emotionally and physically abused me was my father. With the help of counseling and a support group, I learned that I unconsciously sought out relationships with men that fit my prior experience of being criticized and abused. Over the years I had acquired the uncanny ability to find emotionally and physically abusive men. Something inside me operated like sonar or radar where I would choose an abuser even when nice guys were interested in me.

I now have a new sense of myself after working through much anger, fear, guilt and grief. I always knew that I didn't deserve mistreatment on a conscious level of awareness. It has taken much self examination and emotional and spiritual support to begin the healing process which is changing me at depth.

I now realize that my pattern of approval seeking and people pleasing was my attempt to get others to like me in order for me to like myself. Today I like myself, and although I still would prefer everyone to like me, I spend my time taking care of myself and sharing what I find with others instead of trying to meet everyone else's needs in hopes that they might like me and help take care of me. My divorce was unbelievably painful, but the pain brought with it the opportunity to change, uncover and heal all the yucky stuff I had inside me that kept me from being able to relate to myself and others in healthy and productive ways.

JOHN

I have had trouble saying no all my life. During my divorce, my attempt to take care of the world reached new proportions. I became overwhelmed with new activities. My capacity to say yes to every Tom, Dick and Harry exceeded my imagination. Saying yes to everyone was my attempt to avoid feeling what was going on inside my gut.

When I was born, I think I must have come home from the hospital in a blue blanket with a note pinned to the blanket that said, "YOU ARE A MALE AND AS A RESULT OF THIS FACT, YOU ARE PLACED ON EARTH TO TAKE CARE OF THINGS AND PEOPLE -- ESPECIALLY WOMEN -- AND ESPECIALLY WOMEN WHO ARE CRITICAL AND CAN'T BE PLEASED. IN THE EVENT YOU EVER FAIL AND DO NOT TAKE CARE OF ALL THINGS AND ALL PEOPLE -- ESPECIALLY WOMEN -- AND ESPECIALLY WOMEN WHO ARE CRITICAL AND CAN'T BE PLEASED -- YOU MUST FEEL TERRIBLE AND AWFUL ABOUT YOURSELF, TRY HARDER THE NEXT TIME AND PUNISH YOURSELF FOR YOUR FAILURE."

While in counseling, I remembered that my mother had the ability to manipulate my brothers and me (I was the oldest) to feel sad and disappointed when she felt sad and disappointed. Mom felt sad and disappointed most of the time. I erroneously learned at an early age that I was somehow responsible for my mother's feelings and her self worth. Since she felt bad most of the time, I developed a negative self worth and grew up feeling like I was a failure. In order to compensate for my feelings of failure, I tried all the harder to take care of people -- especially women -- and especially women who were critical and who couldn't be pleased (just like Mom). I failed at each attempt. With my increasing load of guilt and frustration, I set myself up for becoming the world's best critic. Since I thought it was my job to make women happy, I got mad when my wife didn't respond to my taking charge of her life. Like any good manipulator, I would try to coerce my wife into happiness through constant fault-finding and criticism about her non-happy choices. She did not appreciate my attempts at forcing my will upon her, and I now see that I was a royal pain in the ass.

I compounded these problems by stuffing and denying my feelings. My wife was always asking me, "How do you feel about that?" or, "How does that make you feel?" She did not realize that I had learned, like all "real" men, the art form of not feeling anything. Since males were not allowed to show their feelings in our family, the best plan of attack was not to have any feelings at all. During therapy, I found out that I had cut my feelings off when I was around 8 or 9 years old. I was not emotionally equipped to be involved in a successful relationship because I was cut off from my feelings and did not have an emotional life to share with my wife. The one emotion that I did express was anger -- or rage. My anger would always come out after I failed to get my wife to act, or react, the way I wanted her to. I told myself that it was her fault because she wasn't allowing me to make her happy, like I needed to in order to fulfill my misguided mission in life.

It has taken a lot of time, sweat and tears, but I believe that I am finally on a track where a healthy relationship with a woman is possible. I first had to learn how to relate to myself in a healthy way which meant that I had to find and recover my lost emotional-feeling nature and make peace with the past. I realize that before I can find "the right person," I must become the right person -- not a perfect human being, but one who understands himself and is willing to live life based upon self examination, honesty, forgiveness and prayer.

BRINGING THE PAST TO LIGHT

Last winter I saw a young boy riding his bicycle in the snow. As he approached an intersection, he tried to stop. He ended up sliding on the snow and fell off his bike. I could tell by watching the fall that he had injured his left arm. He looked like he was going to cry, but as he looked around and saw me looking at him, his facial expression changed. His expression changed from "I'm hurt and I'm going to cry" to "no big deal here, no problem, no sweat." Just like this young boy, we have all learned to swallow our pain and discomfort. We have learned to keep our emotions secretly hidden from view. The problem is that suppressing our feelings and keeping our injuries secret create emotional and spiritual illness. By hiding our past in the depths of our consciousness, we allow emotional wounds from the past to grow and fester. It is through identifying and sharing our experiences and pain that we unravel hidden knots of fear, anger and guilt. If we do not uncover and disclose the heartache and pain of our past, we will continue to wither away and ultimately die of spiritual and emotional suffocation and fatigue. How can we expect a relationship with another person to succeed when we keep ourselves in emotional and spiritual bondage? As long as we remain emotionally imprisoned in the past, our self-centered fears and our attempts to control will continue to result in relationship failure and needless suffering.

By exploring our past we can get a good idea of what "in us" needs fixing. By taking stock of our past experiences, assets and liabilities, we can identify the areas in our life and character traits (that we possess) that need our attention and healing. By bringing the past to light, we will uncover and begin treating emotional wounds that keep us from experiencing closeness and intimacy with ourselves and others.

The recovery process involves going back throughout your life and identifying and disclosing your life story. Recovering from the trauma of divorce, and recovering from life in general, involves exploring and expressing your past experiences -- the good, the bad and the ugly -- all of it. The reason your last relationship didn't work is the same reason your next relationship will fail -- you haven't learned how to do successful relationships yet. The main reason we don't know how to do successful relationships is we have not completed the emotional and spiritual healing work that is necessary in order to heal the emotional wreckage and heartache of the past. As long as we carry around our unresolved emotional baggage from the past, we will be unable to participate effectively in the present. If we are unable to be emotionally present, our attempts at love and intimacy will fail.

There are numerous inventories, value clarification guides, questionnaires and journal-writing formats on the market. Your counselor can help direct you to the self-examination tools that will benefit you. I would recommend that you discuss the inventory guide Jim writes about with your counselor. The point is that we need to examine ourselves and our own histories in order to determine what needs "fixing" inside us.

The following story describes how Jim found an effective way to inventory his healing needs.

JIM

I hate to admit it, but I reached the age of 48 without ever looking closely at my own history or examining my life. When I finally got around to exploring my past in counseling, I saw emotional patterns that made sense. I realized for the first time why I had never been happy in or out of relationships. I was angry at almost everyone I had ever known, and I was full of fear. If you had asked me before I had looked into my past if I had a fear or anger problem, I would have answered, "no," and would have believed that I had answered truthfully.

I also saw why my sexual relationships always started out hot and heavy and ended with avoidance. I had been carrying around a ton of guilt about sex and realized that my introduction to sex involved embarrassment, fear and pain. I am glad that I am making peace with my past. The more I forgive myself and others for what I did or what they did to me, the better I feel about myself and everyone else. Self-searching helped turn on a light with which I began to see the mess that needed to be straightened up.

I began looking at my past by borrowing an inventory guide used by a friend of mine who is a member of Alcoholics Anonymous. (16) My friend described the relief he felt after doing what he called a fourth and fifth step. (17) After talking to my friend, I realized that using his A.A. inventory would probably help me figure out why I had so many difficulties with relationships. The information I wrote out about my past involved five areas. The following is the inventory guide that I used:

1. Name the people, institutions and principles with whom you have been angry. In each instance when you have been angered, list why you got mad and how you were injured.
2. Regarding all the incidents described in your resentment list, describe where you had been selfish, dishonest, self-seeking and frightened -- where were you to blame?
3. Make a list of every time you have ever been afraid and for each instance write out why you were afraid.
4. In regard to past sexual behavior, where have you been selfish, dishonest, or inconsiderate and whom did you hurt and did you unjustifiably arouse jealousy, suspicion or bitterness? Where you were at fault, what should you have done instead?
5. Write on any other subject that has ever caused you emotional pain by identifying the experience -- what happened, how did you feel, and how do you feel now? Write on any other subject that you believe is important.

Identifying and writing about the experiences I had in the past which evoked anger, fear and guilt helped me get a clear picture of my healing needs. It is still hard to believe how unaware I was of my character defects, especially my selfishness and self-centeredness.

2. EXPRESSION/DISCLOSURE

"And ye shall know the truth, and the truth shall make you free." (18)

Any therapist, minister, priest or rabbi worth her or his salt will tell you that talking about your past is an essential part of emotional healing and spiritual growth. The Catholic Church calls this step confession, and therapists call it therapy. No matter what you call it, getting the past "off your chest" frees your heart which otherwise is held prisoner by the hurtful experiences of your past. Freedom comes when these experiences are talked "out" in a safe and non-judgmental atmosphere. Talking about your life story will help you separate fact from fiction and clarify what (inside you) needs healing.

The second step or strategy of the healing process involves expressing out the emotional pain of the past. Jim began his disclosure process by reading what he had written in response to the inventory guide to his counselor.

The following story describes the benefits Gina experienced as she disclosed her past.

GINA

Ten years ago I awoke one morning, looked over at the stranger lying next to me, who was my husband, and experienced an overwhelming sense of aloneness and loss. As painful as that awakening was, it still could not compare to the feelings of emptiness and meaninglessness which I began to experience as I became increasingly aware of the extent to which my life had become focused on the lives of others at the expense of my own needs and feelings. I had forgotten that I even had an identity of my own! In the years that have followed, self-disclosure within a safe and supportive counseling relationship has played a major role in helping me to rediscover and validate my lost self.

When a counselor asked me to write my autobiography several years ago, I was filled with anxiety. I handed it to her with a sense of sadness and resignation. How could she possibly accept me after she found out how awful I really was? It was through her acceptance that I gained the courage to move on with further disclosure and self-discovery. Together we sorted out the pieces of my life, letting go of old shame and pain, while forgiving, affirming and reclaiming parts of myself that I had hidden away and drowned.

At first, disclosure only seemed safe in a counseling relationship where confidentiality was assumed. Later, disclosure in a slightly different sense became an increasingly important part of the way I related to others. As I gained more self-awareness, I became willing and able to present a more authentic self to others. I was able to share both positive and negative feelings and to deal more openly and honestly with conflict. The more acceptance I felt for myself, the more acceptance I felt for others. Gradually my network of supportive relationships began to grow. I was also able to let go of relationships which were not healthy or which perhaps were simply outgrown.

The process of self-disclosure and self-discovery has been paralleled by a process of spiritual discovery and growth. I have experienced a greater sense of connectedness between my true self and the self I present to others and also a greater connectedness in the relationships between myself and others. As this feeling of connectedness has expanded, I have gained an ever-growing serenity and peace.

78

3. ACCEPTANCE AND SURRENDER

The third step in the healing process involves acceptance and surrender. In order to emotionally move on with your life, you need to accept the past and surrender to the fact that what has happened has happened. You may not like what has happened in the past; however, you can't change it. You don't have to like the past in order to accept it. The study and practice of the Serenity Prayer is especially helpful in accepting the past and surrendering to the way life has been up until now: "*God grant me the serenity to accept the things I cannot change, the courage to change the things I can and the wisdom to know the difference.*"

The past cannot be altered. If you can't change it, you need to accept it in order to live in the present. This is a difficult stage to traverse, especially if you enjoy suffering. Accepting the past might mean that you may have to give up complaining about how awful life has been and how terribly you have been treated.

If we don't make a conscious decision to accept, surrender and make peace with the past, we will continue to struggle against it. In our struggle, we will be stuck to the past like Brer Rabbit was stuck to Tar Baby. (19) The more we fight against the past, the more stuck in it we become, eliminating any possibility of finding peace and fulfillment in the present moment.

By identifying the things in the past that hurt (in step one) and telling someone about those experiences (in step two), you will find it easier to accept the past. If you find it difficult to accept something that happened in the past, ask God for the willingness and courage to accept it. Remember you do not have to like what has happened. You do not need to approve of what has happened. You do need to accept what has happened in order to move on with your life. Staying stuck in the past only hurts you.

HENRY THAT S.O.B.

One day a client came into my office and asked me to help her with some estate planning. This client was a gentle lady in her late 70's or early 80's. She presented a calm and pleasant demeanor until we began talking about her family and "HENRY, THAT SON OF A BITCH" (her words). This lady almost broke into a sweat as she started telling me about this nogoodnik named Henry. Henry was her deceased husband. Henry had been dead well over 30 years, but he was alive and well within the confines of my client's thoughts and feelings. As she recounted numerous unpleasantries involving Henry, her face wrinkled and turned red, her lips drew thin and her eyes turned cold. This lady had not accepted, surrendered or made peace with the past. In her refusal to give up her well-rehearsed resentments, she continued to inflict pain on herself over things that happened long ago that involved someone who was six feet under the ground. Are you carrying around a Henry in your head and heart? Now is the time for all of us to let the past be the past.

> *Acceptance and surrender are the two attitudes that open all doors to us. . . Yet they are the most difficult for many of us to acquire. No matter how badly we think life has beaten us, we still cling to the idea that acceptance and surrender are a kind of hopeless giving-in, a weakness of character. Not so! ACCEPTANCE means simply admitting there are things we cannot change. Accepting them puts an end to our futile struggles and frees our thought and energy to work on things that can be changed. Surrender means relinquishing our self-will and accepting God's will and His help. (20)*

4. FORGIVENESS

"You have heard that it was said, 'You shall love your neighbor and hate your enemy.' But I say to you, Love your enemies and pray for those who persecute you. . ." (21)

The fourth step of healing is the forgiveness step. The forgiveness stage is a powerful stage of healing and goes hand in hand with acceptance and surrender. Forgiveness involves forgiving those who have harmed you and forgiving yourself for the injuries you have caused others and yourself. The problem with forgiveness is that it can be practiced prematurely. Before forgiveness will work, you need to identify your anger, frustration or resentment and express the way you feel -- ventilate. Attempting to forgive someone who has harmed you without first identifying and expressing "out" your true feelings is like applying a bandage to a festering sore without first cleaning it out. It might look clean and neat for a while, but underneath the bandage the sore will continue to fester and will ultimately turn to gangrene -- and in the case of resentments, the festering sore will turn into emotional gangrene.

Clients often argue against forgiveness. They simply do not want to forgive someone who has hurt them. Usually these clients will change their minds about forgiveness after they ventilate their hurt and realize that they are continuing to injure only themselves by holding on to their anger and resentment. When you stay angry, you prolong **your** suffering. Staying mad at someone allows the person with whom you are angry to live rent-free in your heart and head. Any person, place or thing you resent controls your emotions. The freedom that comes from forgiveness finds its way into your heart, not theirs.

Forgiveness is no easy matter, and the use of repetitive written affirmations can be helpful. If you want to be free of guilt and resentment, I would recommend that you write the following affirmations 15 times a day for two months.

"I now forgive myself for everything I have ever done or failed to do that has hurt others or myself in any way."

"I now forgive everyone who has injured me or others in any way."

You can tailor forgiveness affirmations to fit specific instances that you feel are appropriate. For example, "I now forgive (insert the person's name) for (insert the event or experience you resent)," or "I now forgive myself for (insert the event or experience you feel guilty about)."

Prayer is our most powerful and productive forgiveness tool. If you find forgiveness difficult or troublesome, it might help to ask God to give you the willingness to forgive yourself or others.

Restitution helps promote self forgiveness. Making personal amends to the people we have hurt (no matter what they have done to us) helps us forgive ourselves and live more freely. I would recommend that you discuss restitution strategy with your counselor before you begin to make amends to those people you believe you have harmed.

So if you are offering your gift at the altar, and there remember that your brother has something against you, leave your gift there before the altar and go; first be reconciled to your brother and then come and offer your gift. (22)

5. GRATITUDE

"Rejoice always, pray constantly, give thanks in all circumstances;
for this is the will of God . . ." (23)

This fifth strategy is the most difficult stage to understand and practice. Spiritual healing is greatly facilitated if you develop a philosophy about the past based upon the premise that the past was good and that you are genuinely grateful for the past. This philosophy is in line with the idea that, ". . .*all things work together for good. . ." (24)*

You do not need to be happy or pleased about the past. You only need to develop a philosophy of gratitude which will empower you to extract meaning and power out of your past experiences. The times in life that seem the most difficult and painful give us the opportunity to grow emotionally and spiritually.

"Cling to the thought that in God's hands the dark past is the greatest
possession you have -- the key to life and happiness for others. With it
you can avert death and misery for them." (25)

If you are willing to take responsibility for your own life and healing, then the process of healing will transform the pain of your past into strength, joy and wisdom. You will see that as a result of your own brokenness, you are now able to help and love others and yourself.

The healing stage of gratitude requires faith and the spiritual understanding and wisdom that:

Without your wounds where would your power be? The angels themselves, cannot help the frightened and bewildered children on earth as can one human being broken on the wheels of life. In love's service only the wounded soldiers can serve. (26)

The point is, the past is full of hurt and pain. Everyone has been hurt and injured in life. It is now up to you to determine whether you are going to use the richness of the past as a target for your complaints and bitterness or a foundation upon which to grow in love and understanding.

A former psychology professor of mine shared the following story one day during class. When he was a young boy, his mother came outside after she heard him crying. He told his mother that his friend had died. His friend was a butterfly that had been working its way out of a cocoon. My professor had tried to help it out of its cocoon, and the butterfly died. His mother told him that what he had tried to do was a very loving thing. She also told him that she thought that maybe the butterfly needed to work itself out of the cocoon by itself in order to gain the strength it needed to fly. Divorce is definitely a cocoon experience. The struggle, darkness, tension, anxiety and conflict that we go through during a divorce provide an opportunity for emotional and spiritual growth. Just as a butterfly springs forth out of its struggle with its cocoon, we have an opportunity to transform into a more loving human being through the metamorphosis that occurs during a divorce. Gratitude is an important stage of spiritual and emotional metamorphosis.

6. GIVING

"Helping others is the foundation stone in your recovery." (27)

The sixth step in the healing formula involves the giving of yourself. Step six is a simple step that will generate profound results. Step six requires that you volunteer yourself into a relationship with another person or a group of people that needs your help. Do not request or expect any return and see what happens. You don't have to look far in order to find people who need your love and support -- nursing homes, local Aids projects, Big Brothers-Big Sisters Programs, hospitals, community centers, etc. Volunteering your gifts of experience, time, energy and money into the lives of others, with no strings attached, will bless your life. You can help heal yourself by helping others heal themselves.

". . . I will have peace of mind in exact proportion to the peace of mind
I bring into the lives of other people." (28)

7. CONTEMPLATIVE PRAYER AND MEDITATION

"But seek ye first the kingdom of God. . ." (29)

". . .the Kingdom of God is within you." (30)

The seventh step of healing is the contemplative prayer or meditation step. Meditation is a form of contemplative prayer that is and has been practiced in Christianity and all other major religions. (31) In order for meditation to be effective, one needs to calm down the mind through the application of the first six steps of emotional and spiritual healing. The emotional clean up work of steps one through six helps set the stage for a meaningful connection with God through meditation.

Contemplative prayer or meditation is our most powerful healing tool. The power of meditation turns fear, anger and guilt into peace, harmony and love. The following is a list of traits or characteristics that evolve from meditation as compared with a fear, anger and guilt based identity:

Traits derived from meditation:	Traits derived from a fear, anger and guilt based identity:
spontaneous	rigid
calm	tense
aware of others	self-centered
generous	selfish
patient	rushed
tolerant	judgmental
assertive	submissive or aggressive

happy and cheerful	depressed, angry, fearful and guilty
joyous	ungrateful
loving	indifferent
committed	avoiding
energetic	tired
cooperative	domineering or compliant
trusting	suspicious
humble	arrogant
willing to change and grow	smug and complacent
forgiving	resentful
committed to spirit	devotion to ego
confident	apprehensive
purposeful	aimless
free from addictions and compulsion	addictive and compulsive
peaceful	apprehensive

The characteristics on the right side of the list generate conflict and turmoil. These characteristics are responsible for the demise of marriages and relationships. The characteristics on the left side of the list promote harmony, peace and love and will help ensure success in every life experience, including marriage and all other forms of relationships.

Conscious contact with God is our ultimate source in healing. Meditation is a skill we can develop that will increase our conscious contact with God and avail to us God's healing power, grace and guidance. Through the daily practice of meditation, you will be "born again" in the sense that a new identity will spring forth from the inner depths of your consciousness. Contemplative prayer will complete the healing of your old fearful, angry and guilty state of consciousness.

Fears melt during the practice of meditation. While fears are real and must be dealt with on the level of personality, fears do not exist on the spiritual plane. You will derive spiritual guidance and direction from meditation. Your life will become more and more meaningful as each meditation brings with it the opportunity for Spirit to infuse your heart and mind. You will begin to understand at depth that ". . .*greater is he that is you, than he that is in the world.*" *(32)* Spirit has always been alive and well inside you. Meditation is a spiritual exercise that allows and encourages Spirit to heal our hearts and direct our minds and actions. The spiritual growth you achieve through meditation will heal the past and ensure successful and loving relationships in your future.

Meditation will strengthen your intuition, which in turn will guide and direct you in the ways of the heart. Feeling and thinking your way into relationships in the past didn't work and led to divorce court. It's time to build relationships upon a spiritual foundation of prayer and meditation.

> *"Man is blind until he achieves insight and he is deaf until he hears the inner voice of his own being." (33)*

If you seriously wanted to learn how to play the guitar or the piano, you would commit yourself to practice the instrument every day. The same is true for meditation. Meditation works best if you practice twice a day: first thing in the morning -- before breakfast, for twenty minutes and for another twenty minutes in the late afternoon to early evening -- before dinner.

At first your feelings and thoughts will not cooperate with your desire to meditate. Your mind will try to convince you that there are many other things you should be doing instead of meditating. Your mind will tell you that you don't have enough time to meditate or that meditation isn't that great of an idea anyway. You may find yourself fidgety and experiencing all sorts of feelings and thoughts when you begin to meditate. Just stick with it -- all the rebellion you will encounter from your thoughts and feelings will subside with time. Our minds are so proud of themselves; they like to make noise all the time. Our minds call attention to our ego, which is a very poor source of insight and inspiration. This is one of the reasons why meditation is so necessary. While the mind is busy clamoring around, we are cut off from conscious contact with God and unable to access spiritual awareness and guidance. Meditation is a process through which our emotional and mental ramblings are calmed -- the volume (conflict and anxiety) is turned down. Those parts of our consciousness that like to keep our minds at work -- our thoughts and feelings -- will resist our initiation into meditation. In time our compulsive thoughts and feelings will loosen their grip on our attention, and daily meditation will become a spiritual and emotional oasis.

Don't expect instant results. One does not achieve spectacular results by going to the gym one day and working out. However, if you go to the gym and work out every day, you will end up with a powerful and healthy body. By turning within every day in meditation, you will build a powerful and healthy spirit. Meditation does spiritually what a methodical bank depositor does financially. By making small deposits over a substantial period of time, a regular depositor builds financial security. By meditating over a substantial period of time, the daily meditator builds up spiritual security. In order to achieve the best results, meditate every day.

HOW TO MEDITATE

If you meditate in a straight-backed chair, keep your feet on the floor, uncross your legs and cup your hands in your lap. If you sit on the floor or in bed, sit cross-legged or with your legs straight out with your back against a wall or other solid surface. Keep your neck, back and your head in a straight line. You will need to keep warm as your body temperature may lower during meditation. Take the phone off the hook, and put your dogs and cats outside the room in which you meditate.

Before beginning, take a few deep breaths and relax. During the twenty minute meditation time, gently focus your mind on a word, phrase or prayer. The following are some words and phrases that you can choose from, or choose one of your own:

Thank you God for your grace;
Thank you God for your guidance and wisdom;

90

Thank you God for your peace and love;

Thank you God for life;

Thank you God;

Thank you Jesus;

Thank you Holy Spirit;

Jesus;

God;

Spirit;

Peace; or

Thy will be done.

Choose a word, phrase or prayer with which you feel comfortable. Two prayers that work well for meditation are the Lord's Prayer or the Prayer of St. Francis. (34) SLOWLY and silently repeat the word, phrase or prayer over and over again during the twenty minutes. If your mind wanders, and it will, gently return your attention to your word, phrase or prayer. Keep bringing your attention back to the object of your meditation. At the end of twenty minutes, spend a few moments in silent prayer, slowly get up and go on your way.

There are many books on contemplative prayer and meditation. The most important part of meditation is doing it. Remember -- you can't do meditation wrong.

Meditation is a spiritual discipline that builds God consciousness slowly but surely. When we meditate, we allow Spirit to awaken in our consciousness. As long as we rely solely upon our thoughts and feelings, we remain spiritually asleep.

As your intuitive connection with Spirit gets stronger, the importance of your personality will lessen. Whereas before you believed (thought and felt) that you needed to depend upon yourself and the outer effects of your personality, under the guidance of Spirit, you will be intuitively guided and directed into new realms of awareness, peace, love and relationships.

Through the continued discipline of meditation, you will no longer be pushed and pulled by obsessive/compulsive likes and dislikes or by the pain of the past. Meditation is a discipline of love as it takes you into closer communion with God and God's guidance, wisdom and power.

In his book Centering Prayer, Basil Pennington writes on the powerful healing qualities of contemplative prayer and meditation:

> *For those who have never had a good grounding experience of caring love, the experience of God in contemplative prayer can be the ground for a wholly new kind of life, giving them the courage to step forward into loving, creative, and satisfying modes of activity. For everyone, to step back periodically and experience such grounding cannot but have a powerful influence on the way he or she relates to self, to God and to all life's activity. (35)*

> *When we experience our true beauty and worth in God's creative and adoptive love, the negativity we are tempted to feel about ourselves melts away and gives place to joy and freedom. Secure in our own true worth, we no longer need to be competitive or jealous or stand on the head of the other to bolster our slumping ego. We can stand in the crowd and not be lost, because we know we are uniquely the object of a divine Love. (36)*

Others have written about the positive impact of meditation:

> *Perhaps one of the greatest rewards of meditation and prayer is the sense of belonging that comes to us. We no longer live in a completely hostile world. We are no longer lost and frightened and purposeless. The moment we begin to see truth, justice, and love as the real and eternal things in life, we are no longer deeply disturbed by all the seeming evidence to the contrary that surrounds us in purely human affairs. We*

know that God lovingly watches over us. We know that when we turn to Him, all will be well with us, here and hereafter. (37)

"Do not be conformed to this world but be ye transformed by the renewal of your mind, that you may prove what is the will of God, what is good and acceptable and perfect. (38)

8. FINDING ONGOING SUPPORT

When I lived in Hawaii, I worked as a clinical director of an alcohol and drug treatment center where I spent most of my time counseling with alcoholics. During treatment, patients attended Alcoholics Anonymous (A.A.) meetings several evenings a week. The treatment facility attempted to impress upon the patients that their success in recovering from alcoholism was dependent upon their participation in A.A. after they left treatment. A large part of the treatment program was designed to expose the patients to A.A. and A.A. literature. The treatment staff attempted to help each patient grasp the A.A. program while in treatment, so when the patients returned home, they would continue their involvement with the A.A. program.

During the last thirteen years, I have counseled with many therapy clients who were members of A.A. and other 12 step organizations such as Alanon, Narcotics Anonymous, Overeaters Anonymous, Sex and Love Addicts Anonymous, Emotions Anonymous and Gamblers Anonymous. It has been my observation that these clients have emotionally healed and spiritually grown much faster than other clients who have not participated in 12 step groups. I have become so impressed with the results achieved by clients who are members of 12 step programs that I recommend 12 step literature to all my counseling clients, whether or not they are involved in 12 step programs. I believe that working through the 12 steps will provide the emotional and spiritual guidance needed to recover from any emotional challenge. One of the main reasons these clients heal faster than other clients is due to the group support they find in 12 step programs.

Finding ongoing support is important for everyone. If your life has been adversely affected by someone's use of alcohol, I would recommend that you try going to some Alanon meetings. If drinking alcohol has caused or is causing problems for you or your family, I would suggest you give Alcoholics Anonymous a try. If overeating or undereating is causing you concern, Overeaters Anonymous may be your answer. I understand there are no dues or fees for membership in 12 step groups. Many clients report that these

95

programs have been especially helpful to them during the crisis of divorce. Some of the benefits of these programs are called the promises. The promises provide an emotional and spiritual environment out of which to grow personally and upon which to build healthy and loving relationships. According to counseling clients who are members of 12 step programs, the following promises come true through the application of the 12 steps to their lives:

> We are going to know a new freedom and a new happiness.
> We will not regret the past nor wish to shut the door on it.
> We will comprehend the word serenity and we will know peace.
> No matter how far down the scale we have gone, we will see how our
> experience can benefit others.
> That feeling of uselessness and self-pity will slip away.
> Our whole attitude and outlook upon life will change.
> Fear of people and of economic insecurity will leave us.
> We will intuitively know how to handle situations which used to baffle
> us.
> We will suddenly realize that God is doing for us what we could not
> do for ourselves. (39)

There are many 12 step programs to choose from. (40) If you cannot find a 12 step program within which to fit and find support, associate with people with interests similar to your own. Companionship is an important ingredient in an ongoing support system. Church affiliation provides support for many people. Singles' groups are springing up in churches and elsewhere. These groups are providing members with the opportunity to be supported and to be of service to others. Clubs and organizations can give members a sense of belonging and purpose. The point is, that we don't have to go it alone. Although it will take a little effort on your part to create a supportive environment in which to live and thrive, your investment in an ongoing support system will pay rich dividends in terms of serenity and a new sense of purpose.

V. WORKING THE 12 STEPS

THE TWELVE STEPS OF ALCOHOLICS ANONYMOUS

1. We admitted we were powerless over alcohol--that our lives had become unmanageable. 2. Came to believe that a Power greater than ourselves could restore us to sanity. 3. Made a decision to turn our will and our lives over to the care of God *as we understood Him.* 4. Made a searching and fearless moral inventory of ourselves. 5. Admitted to God, to ourselves and to another human being the exact nature of our wrongs. 6. Were entirely ready to have God remove all these defects of character. 7. Humbly asked Him to remove our shortcomings. 8. Made a list of all persons we had harmed, and became willing to make amends to them all. 9. Made direct amends to such people wherever possible, except when to do so would injure them or others. 10. Continued to take personal inventory and when we were wrong promptly admitted it. 11. Sought through prayer and meditation to improve our conscious contact with God, *as we understood Him,* praying only for knowledge of His will for us and the power to carry that out. 12. Having had a spiritual awakening as the result of these steps, we tried to carry this message to alcoholics, and to practice these principles in all our affairs. (41)

The program of Alcoholics Anonymous and all other 12 step programs are based upon the following twelve steps. I use these same 12 steps with counseling clients as a framework to follow during their therapy. I invite you to work through these steps with your counselor.

It appears that in the beginning of Alcoholics Anonymous, some people felt that the 12 steps could apply to other problems other than alcoholism. The following quotations appear in early A.A. literature:

> Though the essays which follow were written mainly for members, it is thought by many of A.A.'s friends that these pieces might arouse interest and find application outside A.A. itself. (42)

> I think that psychologically speaking there is a point of advantage the approach that is being made in this (A.A.) movement that cannot be duplicated. I suspect that if it is wisely handled -- and it seems to be in wise and prudent hands -- there are doors of opportunity ahead of this project that may surpass our capacities to imagine. (43)

There are two books that you will need to consult in working the steps: <u>Twelve Steps and Twelve Traditions</u> (hereinafter referred to as the <u>12 & 12</u>) and <u>Alcoholics Anonymous</u> (hereinafter referred to as the <u>Big Book</u>). (44)

STEP ONE -- WE ADMITTED WE WERE POWERLESS OVER OUR ALCOHOL (or whatever your problem may be -- divorce, relationships, food, gambling, drugs, cigarettes, worry, anger etc.) -- THAT OUR LIVES HAD BECOME UNMANAGEABLE. (45)

ASSIGNMEMT:

1. Read the first 50 pages of the <u>Big Book</u> and the first chapter in the <u>12 & 12</u>.

2. Spend one hour writing on how step one applies to your life.

3. Read what you have written to your counselor.

98

STEP TWO -- CAME TO BELIEVE THAT A POWER GREATER THAN OURSELVES COULD RESTORE US TO SANITY.

ASSIGNMENT:

1. Read the next 50 pages of the Big Book and chapter two in the 12 & 12.
2. Spend one hour writing on how step two applies to your life.
3. Read what you have written to your counselor.

STEP THREE -- MADE A DECISION TO TURN OUR WILL AND OUR LIVES OVER TO THE CARE OF GOD AS WE UNDERSTOOD HIM.

ASSIGNMENT:

1. Read the next 50 pages of the Big Book and chapter three in the 12 & 12.
2. Spend one hour writing on how step three applies to your life.
3. Read what you have written to your counselor.

STEP FOUR -- MADE A SEARCHING AND FEARLESS MORAL INVENTORY OF OURSELVES.

ASSIGNMENT:

1. Read the next 50 pages of the Big Book and chapter four in the 12 & 12.
2. Spend as much time as you need in order to write out the information called for in the fourth step inventory guide.
3. Before beginning your fourth step writing, set up a time with your counselor to read what you will write.
4. The following is the information you need to write out for your 4th step inventory:

1. Name the people, institutions and principles with which you have been angry. In each instance when you have been angered, list why you got mad and how you were injured. See the example on page 65 of the Big Book.

2. Regarding all the incidents described in your resentment list, describe where you had been selfish, dishonest, self-seeking and frightened -- where were you to blame?

3. Make a list of every time you have ever been afraid and for each instance write out why you were afraid.

4. In regard to past sexual behavior, where have you been selfish, dishonest, or inconsiderate? Whom did you hurt and did you unjustifiably arouse jealousy, suspicion or bitterness? Where you were at fault, what should you have done instead?

STEP FIVE -- ADMITTED TO GOD, TO OURSELVES, AND TO ANOTHER HUMAN BEING THE EXACT NATURE OF OUR WRONGS.

ASSIGNMENT:

1. Read the next 50 pages of the Big Book and chapter five in the 12 & 12.

2. Add anything you feel is relevant to what you have written for your fourth step inventory.

3. Read what you have written in response to the fourth step inventory guide to your counselor.

Steps 6 through 12. Follow the same procedure for steps 6 through 12. Read the next 50 pages of the Big Book for each step and the corresponding chapter in the 12 & 12. Spend one hour with each step, writing on how the step applies to you. Then read what you have written to your counselor and take the action you need to take in order to carry out the intention of the remaining steps (steps 6, 7, 8, 9, 10, 11 and 12).

The following story has been shared by Anne who has recovered from a variety of emotional and spiritual ailments. Working the 12 steps helped her deal more effectively with relationships and life in general.

ANNE

I am the middle daughter of a schizophrenic mother and an untreated manic-depressive father. My mother did not want me, even when she was pregnant with me. She didn't want me because my father did. As an infant, she didn't hold me and nurture me. She says what a good baby I was. I didn't cry, I didn't care if I was fed or not, held or not, clean or not. I was content just to lie in the crib all the time.

When I was little, I used to think I had two mothers -- the mean, pretend mother at home and the beautiful loving one in public. I actually thought they were two separate people who looked alike. I couldn't figure when or how the switch was made or where the mean one kept the good one hidden while at home. I'd hunt for her so I could free her. I always wanted to ask the good one where she was hidden at home. I never did. I don't know why.

My father was pretty elusive, too. He was a moody, solemn, dark, scary man who didn't talk for days, weeks into months. The one you couldn't talk around. The one who would follow you around and just stare at you. The one who could back-hand you so hard your body would lift from the floor and hit the wall behind you. The one who would walk away as you lay on the floor too shocked to speak, too numb to cry. That was his depressive side. When the depression lifted, he would talk about death, hell, sins, torture, rape, suicide and evil.

The other swing was a happy soul who bought things -- five boats one time, two new cars another, and he refurnished the house a couple of times. This guy wasn't around much -- a mixed blessing I suppose. Anyway, there was this other guy in the middle. He

101

was my hero. He liked me and took me places with him -- the lumber yard, a hardware store, not little girl places but I was with him and that's all that mattered.

My parents were pretty normal in public. In the 1950's they were a typical couple. My father always worked and provided an average lifestyle. My mother was active in P.T.A., was a room mother, a Girl Scout leader, a Sunday school teacher. My friends liked my parents. The neighbors did too.

But, I knew something was wrong. Actually I didn't know it. I felt it. I thought it must be me. I thought there was something inalterably wrong with me. I tried to improve. I made good grades, behaved well in public, minded my friends' parents, but in my private life I was a thief. I shoplifted from age 6 to 29. I never got caught. I started smoking at age 6 and smoked regularly through grade school and through life until I was 30. I started drinking at age 14. I got drunk with friends nearly every weekend until I was 21. Then I started smoking pot regularly until I was 24. I was never caught.

I drove drunk regularly too. I was never caught. I abused food all my life. I saved my allowance and stole money from the collection plate at church and bought fine chocolates with the money.

I joined my first 12-Step program when I was 33. I had gained 30 pounds in one month when I was working on my Master's thesis, and I was suicidally depressed about it. I thought I would learn to live fat and happy. The woman who spoke at my first O.A. meeting became my sponsor. She was the first person with whom I had an honest relationship.

As I worked the steps and exposed hidden parts of myself to her, I learned about who I was. As an adolescent instead of individuating and becoming more me, I became who my peers were or I ceased existing by being drunk. So at age 33 I had to find me and become me. I created me out of all the little fragments of myself that I left along the way as I grew up -- the pieces I was ashamed of, that I rejected and forgot about, the parts torn from me with bloody, awful pain.

With the steps, with my sponsor, with the fellowship of the group I began to see my life in segments -- the least painful at first. My most functional relationships were examined by me. They hardly existed. I was simply an extension of my friends. I had few independent thoughts. I didn't have many feelings. I lived without honesty because I couldn't separate truth from fantasy.

My sponsor and I were developing my first real relationship. She didn't care what I had done or failed to do. She accepted me as I was. I began to trust her because she awakened trust in me. I began to trust the group. I began to trust me. Then I could probe a little deeper into my heart. I could risk feeling a little more.

I started sponsoring other people and found out that I wasn't as uncommon as I had thought. I became less embarrassed to be me and more willing to expose who I truly was to others so they could heal too.

As I grew into greater awareness, my life didn't change in big ways. I kept my same profession, retained my friendships, lived in the same place, but I had joy in my existence. I felt more alive. I had courage, and I felt love for the first time, not sexual attraction, but real, deep-down love. I understood that love to be a power greater than me. It was the love of God flowing to me and through me, abundantly, non-exlusionarily.

I started going to Alanon. There I got in touch with more painful memories. I remembered beatings I received as a girl and youth from my mother. But mostly I remembered the pain of the absence of love. I had never mattered to anyone. At least I had not been aware of mattering to anyone. In the program I mattered to a lot of people. I didn't matter to them because of my successes. I mattered to them because of my spirit. I was loved. As I healed more in this program, I went on to Adult Children of Alcoholics. I always went there as an adult, but when I walked through the doors -- I became a child. There I recaptured the fragments of a splintered little girl. I remembered sexually abusive incidents with my father. I remembered them with my mother too. I talked about them at my Alanon group because I knew I was safe there, safe to expose those horrors, safe to feel the pain, safe to lay my heart open and feel the healing power of love. I was safer with that group than I was alone. I knew I would be believed. I knew I would be understood. I knew I wouldn't be blamed. I trusted.

As the years have rolled on, I've learned to trust people outside the program too. I have close friends who don't exploit me, who want me to be me and not just more of them. My friendships now are based on truth, self-disclosure, mutual trust, mutual admiration. We are bonded by love and not in bondage by fear or necessity. We are free to be wholly who we are. We can express our best and our worst and still be respected, loved and honored.

My sponsor died last year. While it was one of the most heartbreaking experiences of my life, it was also one of the most beautiful. She didn't die alone or with people there out of obligation. She was surrounded by program people who loved her and each other. She was surrounded by love, laughter, music, prayer, peace and security. She went out of the world the way all people should enter in: with safety, value, and rejoicing in their lives, their very being.

Program people have a fellowship, a kinship. They are a safe harbor in the storms of life.

With all of the love and understanding that I have received, that I have been allowed and encouraged to give -- I have healed. I'm a whole person. I do not hold my parents in judgment or damnation. I see them as broken, fragmented, sad people. I forgive them because they were never guilty. They weren't accountable. I pray they find their way to the freedom I experience.

FINAL THOUGHTS

Back in the 50's and 60's, people were talking about inferiority complexes. In the 70's and 80's, the buzz words were "low-self esteem." Now in the 90's we are talking about "co-dependency," the "inner child" and "dysfunctional families." The common denominator in all these psychological descriptions is emotional pain and suffering. The human emotional and spiritual condition hasn't really changed much although we continually develop new vocabularies to describe the fear, anger and guilt that continue to plague us all.

There are many theories about why we are the way we are and how we can emotionally and spiritually heal and recover. I believe that the ideas and suggestions contained in this book can help you create a better life for yourself. I hope you and your horse have found what you were looking for during your ride through this book. May God bless you as you continue on your journey. HAPPY TRAILS.

Abandon yourself to God as you understand God. Admit your fault to Him and to your fellows. Clear away the wreckage of your past. Give freely of what you find and join us. We shall be with you in the Fellowship of the Spirit, and you will surely meet some of us as you trudge the Road of Happy Destiny. May God bless you and keep you -- until then. (46)

FOOTNOTES

All Biblical quotations are taken from the King James Version unless otherwise indicated.

(1)   Twelve Steps and Twelve Traditions (The A.A. Grapevine, Inc., and Alcoholics Anonymous Publishing [now known as Alcoholics Anonymous World Services, Inc.], copyright 1952), Library of Congress Catalog No. 53-5454, p. 53. This quotation and other brief quotations are reprinted with the permission of Alcoholics Anonymous World Services, Inc. Permission to reprint these quotations or other material herein, does not mean that A.A. has reviewed or approved the content of this publication nor that A.A. agrees with the views expressed herein. A.A. is a program of recovery from alcoholism--use of the Twelve Steps in connection with programs and activities which are patterned after A.A., but which address other problems, does not imply otherwise.

(2)   Genesis 3:12-3:13

(3)   1 Kings 12:12

(4)   Luke 17:21

(5)   Matthew 6:33

(6)   1 John 4:4

(7)   Proverbs 3:5

(8)   Matthew 6:33

(9)   1 Kings 12:12

(10)   Psalms 46:10

(11)   Niebuhr, Reinhold, "Prayer for Serenity" --

> *God grant me the serenity to accept the things I cannot change, courage to change the things I can and the wisdom to know the difference. Living one day at a time, enjoying one moment at a time. Accepting hardship as a pathway to peace. Taking, as Jesus did, this sinful world as it is, not as I would have it. Trusting that You will make all things right if I surrender to Your will. So That I may be reasonably happy in this life and supremely happy with You forever in the next. AMEN.*

(12)   For information on Alanon write: Al-Anon Family Group Headquarters, Inc., P.O. Box 862, Midtown Station, New York, NY 10018-0862, or call 212/302-7240.

(13)   In order to contact Alcoholics Anonymous, consult your local telephone directory or contact: Alcoholics Anonymous, P.O. Box 459, Grand Central Station, New York, NY 10163.

(14)   Matthew 5:9

(15)   For information on Re-evaluation Counseling, write: Rational Island Publishers, P.O. Box 2081, Main Office Station, Seattle, WA 98111.

(16)   The inventory guide referred to is found in <u>Alcoholics Anonymous</u>, (Alcoholics Anonymous World Services, Inc., copyright 1939, 1955, 1976), Library of Congress Catalog Card No. 76-4029, p. 64-71.

(17)   Ibid. p. 58-71; Also see p. 42-62, <u>Twelve Steps and Twelve Traditions</u> [see endnote 1]

(18)   John 8:32

(19)   Brer Rabbit and Tar Baby were two characters in a Walt Disney motion picture, "Song of the South."

(20)   <u>One Day At A Time In Al-Anon</u>, (Reprinted with permission from Al-Anon Family Group Headquarters, Inc., New York, New York 10018, copyright 1973, Library of Congress Card No. 72-85153, p. 76.

(21)   Matthew 5:43-44 (New Oxford Annotated Bible)

(22)   Matthew 5:23-24 (New Oxford Annotated Bible)

(23)   1 Thessalonians 5:16-18 (New Oxford Annotated Bible)

(24)   Romans 8:28

(25)   <u>Alcoholics Anonymous</u>, (Alcoholics Anonymous World Services, Inc., copyright 1939, 1955, 1976), Library of Congress Catalog Card No. 76-4029, p. 124

(26)   Wilder, Thornton

(27)   <u>Alcoholics Anonymous</u>, [see endnote 25], p. 97

(28)   <u>Alcoholics Anonymous</u>, [see endnote 25], p. 551

(29)   Matthew 6:33

(30)   Luke 17:21

(31)   See Pennington, M. Basil, <u>Centering Prayer</u> (Doubleday Publishers, A Division of Bantam, Doubleday, Dell Publishing Group, Inc., New York, New York), 1982, Easwaran, Eknath, <u>Meditation, An Eight-Point Program</u> (Nilgiri Press, Petaluma, California), 1978, Kaplan, Aryeh, <u>Jewish Meditation, A Practical Guide</u> (Schocken Books, New York), 1985

(32)   1 John 4:4

(33)   Einstein, Albert

(34)   "The Lord's Prayer" --

> *Our Father which art in heaven.*
> *Hallowed be Thy name.*
> *Thy kingdom come.*
> *Thy will be done on earth,*
> *As it is in heaven.*
> *Give us this day our daily bread.*
> *And forgive us our trespasses*
> *As we forgive those who trespass against us.*
> *And lead us not into temptation.*
> *But deliver us from evil;*
> *For Thine is the kingdom*
> *And the power, and the glory, forever, Amen.*

"The Prayer of Saint Francis" --

> *Lord, make me an instrument of thy peace.*
> *Where there is hatred, let me sow love;*
> *Where there is injury, pardon;*
> *Where there is doubt, faith;*
> *Where there is despair, hope;*
> *Where there is darkness, light;*
> *Where there is sadness, joy.*
>
> *O divine Master, grant that I may not so much seek*
> *To be consoled as to console,*
> *To be understood as to understand,*
> *To be loved as to love;*
> *For it is in giving that we receive;*
> *It is in pardoning that we are pardoned;*
> *It is in dying [to self] that we are born to eternal life.*

(35)   Pennington, M. Basil, <u>Centering Prayer</u>, (Reprinted with permission from Doubleday a Division of Bantam, Doubleday, Dell Publishing Group, Inc., New York, New York), 1982, p. 126

(36)   Pennington, M. Basil, Centering Prayer, [see endnote 35], p. 127-128

(37)   Twelve Steps and Twelve Traditions [see endnote 1]

(38)   Romans 12:2 (New Oxford Annotated Bible)

(39)   Alcoholics Anonymous, [see endnote 25], p. 83-84. The promises are printed in a different format than are found in Alcoholics Anonymous and therefore are an adaptation.

(40)   For a list of Twelve-Step Organizations, contact Alcoholics Anonymous, P.O. Box 459, Grand Central Station, New York, NY 10163.

(41)   The Twelve Steps of Alcoholics Anonymous. The Twelve Steps are reprinted with permission of Alcoholics Anonymous World Services, Inc.

(42)   Twelve Steps and Twelve Traditions, [see endnote 1], p. 15

(43)   Alcoholics Anonymous, [see endnote 25], p. 574

(44)   Twelve Steps and Twelve Traditions, [see endnote 1], Alcoholics Anonymous, [see endnote 25]

(45)   The first five steps of the Twelve Steps appearing on pages 98-100 are reprinted and adapted with permission of Alcoholics Anonymous World Services, Inc.

(46)   Alcoholics Anonymous, [see endnote 25], p. 164

APPENDIX A

BIBLIOGRAPHY

GENERAL:

1. Creative Divorce, Krantzler, Mel; M. Evans and Company, Inc., 1974.

2. Marital Separation, Weiss, Robert S.; Basic Books, Inc., 1975.

3. Untying The Knot: A Guide to Civilized Divorce, Bernard, Janine M. and Hackney, Harold; Winston Press, 1983.

4. The Dance of Anger, Lerner, Harriet; Harper and Row, 1985.

5. Crazy Time: Surviving Divorce, Trafford, Abigail; Bantam Books, 1982.

6. When Bad Things Happen to Good People, Kushner, Harold S.; Avon Books, 1981.

7. Intimate Strangers: Men and Women Together, Rubin, Lillian B.; Harper-Colophon Books, 1983.

8. In a Different Voice, Gilligan, Carol; Harvard University Press, 1982.

CHILD CARE ISSUES:

9. Surviving the Breakup, Wallerstein, Judith S. and Kelley, Joan B.; Basic Books, 1980.

10. Second Chances: Men, Women & Children A Decade After Divorce, Wallerstein, Judith S. and Blakeslee, Sandra; Ticknor & Fields, 1889.

11. Mom's House, Dad's House, Making Joint Custody Work, Ricci, I.; MacMillan & Co., 1981.

12. Joint Custody and Shared Parenting, Folberg, Jay, ed.; Bureau of National Affairs, Inc., The Association of Family Conciliation Courts, 1984.

13. Divorce Is A Growing Up Problem: A Book About Divorce For Young Children and Their Parents, Sinberg, Janet; Avon Books, 1978.

BUSINESS AND FINANCE:

14. Women, Divorce, and Money, Rogers, Mary; McGraw-Hill, 1981.

15. Handbook of Tax and Financial Planning for Divorce and Separation, Zipp, A.; Prentice Hall, 1985.

16. The Divorce Revolution, Weitzman, Lenore; Free Press, 1985.

AFTER DIVORCE:

17. Step-families: A Guide to Working With Stepparents and Stepchildren, Visher, Emily B. and John S.; Mazel Books, 1979.

18. Going It Alone, Weiss, Robert S.; Basic Books, Inc., 1979.

NEGOTIATING AGREEMENTS:

19. Getting To Yes, Fisher, Roger and Ury, William; Penguin Books, 1981.

OTHER:

20. The Road Less Traveled, Peck, M. Scott; Touchstone Books, 1978.

21. Human Side of Human Beings, Jackins, Harvey; Rational Island Publishers, 1965.

22. Meditation, An Eight-Point Plan, Easwaran, Eknath; Nilgiri Press, 1978.

CASSETTE TAPES

1. "The Art of Healing Yourself," Wear, William A., Jr., Insight Productions, 1983*

2. "The Meditation Process," Wear, William A., Jr., Insight Productions, 1987*

• To order these cassettes or a free brochure, write:
   Insight Productions
   P.O. Box 50185
   Springfield, MO 65805-0185

APPENDIX B

The following is some of the information contained in the brochure <u>Divorce Mediation</u> that is used in our office. For additional information on mediation or mediators in your community, write the Academy of Family Mediators, P.O. Box 10501, Eugene, Oregon, or call (503) 345-1205.

QUESTIONS & ANSWERS
<u>ABOUT DIVORCE MEDIATION</u>

What Is Divorce Mediation?

Divorce mediation is an informal voluntary process that allows a couple to work out an agreement in such areas as child custody and visitation, property division, child support and spousal maintenance -- with assistance from an impartial mediator. The goal of mediation is to settle these issues in a manner advantageous for the parties and the children, taking into account the interests of all concerned. The process seeks to promote cooperation and minimizes the unnecessary frustration and anger that too often accompany divorce.

What Is A Mediator?

A mediator who specializes in divorce and family mediation generally has an advanced degree in law, mental health, or both. In addition to having a thorough understanding of the specific substantive issues which must be addressed in a divorce settlement, professional mediators have had extensive training in conflict resolution theory and skills. The mediator's responsibility is to facilitate direct communication between the spouses in order to resolve the child care, property division, and financial issues that must be addressed in a settlement.

Will Mediation Save The Marriage?

The mediator does not attempt to pursue a reconciliation of the parties; mediation is not therapy.

Mediation is most effective when both parties acknowledge the divorce is a likely reality. If both parties are still uncertain as to the wisdom of a divorce, we recommend talking to a qualified marriage counselor.

What Are The Advantages Of Mediation?

● The parties maintain control over and take responsibility for making decisions on personal matters that directly affect them and their children.

● The process of mediation allows the divorcing couple to negotiate the terms of an agreement so that the settlement will take into consideration everyone's interests.

● Reaching an agreement through mediation often reduces the tension, anger, and destruction that sometimes accompany the traditional divorce process.

● When there are children involved, the divorcing spouses continue to be parents even though the marriage has been dissolved. The experience in mediation -- of reaching a mutually acceptable agreement on issues, such as distribution of parental responsibilities, time spent with the children, and educational and medical decisions -- is helpful in assuring continued cooperation between the divorcing spouses in their roles as parents.

- The cost of mediated settlement can be less than a traditional divorce negotiated through two separate attorneys, especially if the divorce is contested.

Do I Still Need An Attorney?

Yes. Mediators do not act as attorneys and do not give legal advice. The rule of mediation that most mediators have adopted requires each person to consult with his or her attorney at some point in the mediation process and to review the settlement agreement with his or her own legal counsel. The legal review is not a duplication of the mediation process, but rather it serves to protect both parties and assures that the proposed agreement is legally sound.

What Happens After We Agree On The Issues?

When agreement is reached, the mediator drafts a plain-language memorandum clearly setting forth the terms. The memorandum is then reviewed by both parties with their respective attorneys. The attorneys formally prepare and present the agreement to the court on behalf of the parties at a non-contested hearing set at the convenience of the parties.

How Long Does The Process Take?

Generally, mediation sessions last from an hour to an hour and a half. When child custody, real estate, property, and private business matters need to be resolved -- settlement may take from eight to twelve meetings. In less complex cases, couples may reach agreement in only three or four meetings.

How Much Will It Cost?

Most mediators charge for services at an hourly rate. Mediation does not eliminate the cost of retaining an attorney, but by working out your own terms to the settlement agreement, mediation often results in lower overall costs of the divorce.

Mediator's Qualifications

Here at Family Mediation Associates, we require all mediators to complete: (1) an advanced degree in law, counseling, or behavioral sciences; (2) forty hours of specialized training in divorce and family mediation, and to continue their involvement and education in the field of their specialty and mediation.

APPENDIX C

The following is some of the information contained in the Rules Of Mediation that is used in our office. For additional information on mediation or mediators in your community, write the Academy of Family Mediators, P.O. Box 10501, Eugene, Oregon, or call (503) 345-1205.

RULES OF MEDIATION

1.   **Legal Counsel and Legal Advice**

   a.   THE MEDIATOR IS NOT ACTING AS AN ATTORNEY AND WILL NOT, UNDER ANY CIRCUMSTANCES, GIVE LEGAL ADVICE TO EITHER CLIENT. BOTH CLIENTS ARE ADVISED TO SEEK THEIR OWN LEGAL COUNSEL DURING THE MEDIATION PROCEEDINGS.

   b.   The mediator may give legal information to both clients as may be necessary for the parties to make informed decisions.

   c.   Each client is encouraged to seek the advice of independent and separate legal counsel during the mediation process with regard to his or her individual legal rights and responsibilities.

   d.   The clients agree that no legal action of any kind will be taken by either of them during the course of mediation, except with the express agreement of the other client and the mediator. Further, if either or both clients have retained counsel prior to mediation, they shall be obligated to direct their respective attorneys, in writing, that no action is to be taken on their case while the matter is in mediation.

117

2. Communications with the Mediator

The clients will not communicate or meet with the mediator concerning matters in mediation except in the presence of each other during a mediation session unless the parties expressly agree beforehand that such communication may be helpful and appropriate to reaching settlement.

3. Third Party Involvement

To facilitate the mediation process, the clients shall refrain from discussing the matters in mediation with friends, relatives or others. However, they are encouraged to consult with legal counsel, mental health professionals, and/or clergy.

4. Full Disclosure

a.   Each client shall fully and completely disclose in good faith to the other person and the mediator all information and writings, such as financial statements, income tax returns, pension and/or profit sharing plans, or any other documentation which the mediator requests.

b.   The preparation of budgets and financial statements by each client is an essential part of the mediation process. If either client shall fail or refuse to prepare these documents adequately, the mediator shall have the duty to suspend or, if required, terminate the mediation process.

5. Transfers of Property During Mediation

During the mediation process, neither of the clients shall transfer, encumber, conceal, sell, or in any other way dispose of any tangible or intangible property except in the usual course of business or for the necessities of life. In addition, expenditures made by either client outside regular monthly expenses shall be disclosed prior to expenditure.

6. Confidentiality of the Mediation Process

Contents of the mediation file, or for that matter, any information about clients, even clients' identities, will not be disclosed by any person in this office, without prior consent of both clients or unless compelled by law.

APPENDIX D

The following is some of the information contained in the <u>Agreement For Mediation</u> that is used in our office.

<u>AGREEMENT FOR MEDIATION</u>

This is an agreement to enter into mediation to resolve all issues related to an anticipated separation, separation or post-dissolution dispute which has already occurred. It is the desire of the clients to resolve all such issues without engaging in an adversarial contest. The clients employ FAMILY MEDIATION ASSOCIATES to assist them in resolving the issues between them.

Both clients agree as follows:

1. SELECTION OF MEDIATOR. The clients appoint and retain FAMILY MEDIA-TION ASSOCIATES to mediate all issues relating to the dissolution of their marriage, motion to modify, or related matter. It is understood that the mediator is not a judicial officer of the state and has no authority beyond that conferred by agreement of the clients.

2. PROCEDURE. It is anticipated that the clients and mediator will meet together for six to nine mediation sessions from one to one and one-half hours each, though the number of sessions and their length may vary depending on circumstances and complexities. No other person shall be present except by mutual agreement. The mediator shall prepare a proposed agreement of all issues relating to the clients' circumstances and shall present the agreement to the clients for discussion. If the clients agree to its terms, the clients may take the agreement to their individual attorneys.

3.	NOT BINDING. Even though both clients intend to complete the mediation and sign the mediated Agreement, it is understood that either party may withdraw from the mediation process at anytime prior to signing a final Agreement, which will be drafted by the clients' attorneys. Once a formal Agreement is signed by each, it shall be contractually binding on the clients and may be submitted to the Court for approval and incorporation in to the decree of dissolution or judgment.

4.	FULL DISCLOSURE. Each client shall fully and honestly disclose all information and writings, such as financial statements, budgets, income tax returns, etc., as requested by the mediator and all information required by the opposite client if the mediator finds that the disclosure is appropriate to the mediation process and that the disclosure will aid the clients in reaching a settlement. The clients understand that the final Agreement, even if incorporated into the Court's decree, may be set aside if full disclosure is not made.

5.	CHILDREN. Should the parties have children of their marriage or adopted by them, the best interests of the children shall be of paramount concern within the reality of the dissolution of the marital relationship.

6.	CONFIDENTIALITY OF THE MEDIATION PROCESS. The mediation process is confidential. Clients expressly understand and agree that any statements made during the mediation process by either client about any matter shall be considered confidential. Further, clients understand and agree that insofar as the mediation process is directed towards the settlement of issues which might otherwise be the subject of litigation, statements made by either client during the process are intended to be taken as being in furtherance of settlement, and therefore not admissible as evidence in Court. Further, in signing this Agreement, clients understand and agree to be foreclosed and barred from: repeating any statement made by the other person; requesting the production of any notes, documents, or tapes made by the mediator; or, requesting the testimony of the mediator with regard to any part of the mediation process in Court or any other legal process.

7. RULES OF MEDIATION. Both clients have been provided copies of the Rules of Mediation and understand that those Rules are made a part of this Agreement, and that in agreeing to mediate, both clients are obligated to follow those Rules in good faith.

8. NEUTRALITY OF MEDIATOR. It is understood that the mediator must remain neutral in all contacts with the clients and that the mediator will champion the interests of neither over the other. It is further understood that the mediator is not employed as an attorney to represent either or both of the clients or their children and will <u>NOT</u> give any legal advice.

APPENDIX E

MISSOURI STATUTES

LEGAL REQUIREMENTS FOR A DIVORCE

Section 452.305 of the Revised Statutes of Missouri (effective January 1, 1974) sets forth the requirements for a divorce (dissolution of marriage):

452.305 Decree of dissolution, grounds for -- legal separation, when

1.   The circuit court shall enter a decree of dissolution of marriage if

    (1) The court finds that one of the parties has been a resident of this state, or is a member of the armed services who has been stationed in this state, for ninety days next preceding the commencement of the proceeding and that thirty days have elapsed since the filing of the petition;

    (2) The court finds that there remains no reasonable likelihood that the marriage can be preserved and therefore the marriage is irretrievably broken; and

    (3) To the extent it has jurisdiction to do so, the court has considered, approved, or made provision for child custody, the support of any child of the marriage who is entitled to support, the maintenance of either spouse, and the disposition of property.

2.   If a party requests a decree of legal separation rather than a decree of dissolution of marriage, the court shall grant the decree in that form.

WHO GETS WHAT? PROPERTY DISTRIBUTION

Section 452.330 of the Revised Statutes of Missouri (effective January 1, 1974, amended by legislature 1984, 1988) sets out the factors the court considers regarding property distribution:

452.330 Disposition of property, factors to be considered

1. In a proceeding for dissolution of the marriage or legal separation, or in a proceeding for disposition of property following dissolution of the marriage by a court which lacked personal jurisdiction over the absent spouse or lacked jurisdiction to dispose of the property, the court shall set apart to each spouse his nonmarital property and shall divide the marital property in such proportions as the court deems just after considering all relevant factors including:

    (1) The economic circumstances of each spouse at the time the division of property is to become effective, including the desirability of awarding the family home or the right to live therein for reasonable periods to the spouse having custody of any children;

    (2) The contribution of each spouse to the acquisition of the marital property, including the contribution of a spouse as homemaker;

    (3) The value of the nonmarital property set apart to each spouse;

    (4) The conduct of the parties during the marriage; and

    (5) Custodial arrangements for minor children.

2. For purposes of sections 452.300 to 452.415 only, "marital property" means all property acquired by either spouse subsequent to the marriage except:

    (1) Property acquired by gift, bequest, devise, or descent;

    (2) Property acquired in exchange for property acquired prior to the marriage or in exchange for property acquired by gift, bequest, devise, or descent;

(3) Property acquired by a spouse after a decree of legal separation;

(4) Property excluded by valid written agreement of the parties; and

(5) The increase in value of property acquired prior to the marriage or pursuant to subdivisions (1) to (4) of this subsection, unless marital assets including labor, have contributed to such increases and then only to the extent of such contributions.

3. All property acquired by either spouse subsequent to the marriage and prior to a decree of legal separation or dissolution of marriage is presumed to be marital property regardless of whether title is held individually or by the spouses in some form of co-ownership such as joint tenancy, tenancy in common, tenancy by the entirety, and community property. The presumption of marital property is overcome by a showing that the property was acquired by a method listed in subsection 2 of this section.

4. Property which would otherwise be nonmarital property shall not become marital property solely because it may have become commingled with marital property.

5. The court's order as it affects distribution of marital property shall be a final order not subject to modification; provided, however, that orders intended to be qualified domestic relations orders affecting pension, profit sharing and stock bonus plans pursuant to the U.S. Internal Revenue Code shall be modifiable only for the purpose of establishing or maintaining the order as a qualified domestic relations order or to revise or conform its terms so as to effectuate the expressed intent of order.

6. A certified copy of any decree of court affecting title to real estate may be filed for record in the office of the recorder of deeds of the county and state in which the real estate is situated by the clerk of the court in which the decree was made. Such filing fees shall be taxed as costs in the cause.

WILL THE COURT AWARD ALIMONY?

Section 452.335 of the Revised Statutes of Missouri (effective January 1, 1974, amended by legislature 1988) sets forth the criteria which must be met before a court is authorized to award either party alimony (maintenance):

452.335 Maintenance order, findings required for -- termination date, may be modified, when

1. In a proceeding for non-retroactive invalidity, dissolution of marriage or legal separation, or a proceeding for maintenance following dissolution of the marriage by a court which lacked personal jurisdiction over the absent spouse, the court may grant a maintenance order to either spouse, but only if it finds that the spouse seeking maintenance:

    (1) Lacks sufficient property, including marital property apportioned to him, to provide for his reasonable needs; and
    (2) Is unable to support himself through appropriate employment or is the custodian of a child whose condition or circumstances make it appropriate that the custodian not be required to seek employment outside the home.

2. The maintenance order shall be in such amounts and for such periods of time as the court deems just, and after considering all relevant factors including:

    (1) The financial resources of the party seeking maintenance, including marital property apportioned to him, and his ability to meet his needs independently, including the extent to which a provision for support of a child living with the party includes a sum for that party as custodian;
    (2) The time necessary to acquire sufficient education or training to enable the party seeking maintenance to find appropriate employment;
    (3) The comparative earning capacity of each spouse;
    (4) The standard of living established during the marriage;

(5) The obligations and assets, including the marital property apportioned to him and the separate property of each party;

(6) The duration of the marriage;

(7) The age, and the physical and emotional condition of the spouse seeking maintenance;

(8) The ability of the spouse from whom maintenance is sought to meet his needs while meeting those of the spouse seeking maintenance;

(9) The conduct of the parties during the marriage; and

(10) Any other relevant factors.

3. The maintenance order shall state if it is modifiable or non-modifiable. The court may order maintenance which includes a termination date. Unless the maintenance order which includes a termination date is non-modifiable, the court may order the maintenance decreased, increased, terminated, extended, or otherwise modified based upon a substantial and continuing change of circumstances which occurred prior to the termination date of the original order.

CHILD SUPPORT -- HOW MUCH?

The Missouri Supreme Court recently enacted Rule 88 (effective January 1, 1974, current Rule 88 adopted October 2, 1989) which governs child support. Prior to adoption of Rule 88, Section 452.340 of the Revised Statutes of Missouri (effective January 1, 1974, amended by legislature 1988, 1989, 1990) provided guidance to courts regarding the issue of child support. Both Section 452.340 and Supreme Court Rule 88 are set out below:

452.340 Child support, how allocated -- factors to be considered -- abatement or termination of support, when -- payments may be made directly to child, when -- child support guidelines, rebuttable assumption

1. In a proceeding for dissolution of marriage, legal separation or child support, the court may order either or both parents owing a duty of support to a child of the marriage to pay an amount reasonable or necessary for his support, including an award retroactive to the date of filing the petition, without regard to marital misconduct, after considering all relevant factors including:

    (1) The financial needs and resources of the child;
    (2) The financial resources and needs of the parents;
    (3) The standard of living the child would have enjoyed had the marriage not been dissolved;
    (4) The physical and emotional condition of the child, and his educational needs.

2. The obligation of the noncustodial parent to make support payments shall abate, in whole or in part, for such periods of time in excess of thirty consecutive days that the custodial parent has voluntarily relinquished physical custody of a child to the noncustodial parent, notwithstanding any periods of visitation or temporary custody pursuant to a decree of dissolution or legal separation or any modification thereof.

3. Unless the circumstances of the child manifestly dictate otherwise and the court specifically so provides, the obligation of a parent to make child support payments shall terminate when the child:

    (1) Dies;
    (2) Marries;
    (3) Enters active duty in the military;
    (4) Becomes self-supporting, provided that the custodial parent has relinquished the child from parental control by express or implied consent; or
    (5) Reaches age eighteen or graduates from a secondary school, whichever later occurs, unless the provisions of subsection 4 or 5 of this section apply.

4. If the child is physically or mentally incapacitated from supporting himself and insolvent and unmarried, the court may extend the parental support obligation past the child's eighteenth birthday.

5. If the child is enrolled in an institution of vocational or higher education not later than October first following graduation from a secondary school and so long as the child continues to attend such institution of vocational or higher education, the parental support obligation shall continue until the child completes his education, or until the child reaches the age of twenty-two, whichever first occurs. If the child is enrolled in such institution, the child or obligated parent may petition the court to amend the order to direct the obligated parent to make the payments directly to the child. As used in this section, an "institution of vocational education" means any post-secondary training or schooling for which the student is assessed a fee and attends classes regularly. "Higher education" means any junior college, college, or university at which the child attends classes regularly.

6. A court may abate, in whole or in part, any future obligation of support or may transfer the custody of one or more children if it finds:

    (1) That a custodial parent has, without good cause, failed to provide visitation or temporary custody to the noncustodial parent pursuant to the terms of a decree of dissolution, legal separation or modifications thereof; and

    (2) That the noncustodial parent is current in payment of all support obligations pursuant to the terms of a decree of dissolution, legal separation or modification thereof. The court may also award reasonable attorney fees to the prevailing party.

7. Not later than October 13, 1989, the Missouri supreme court shall have in effect a rule establishing guidelines by which any award of child support shall be made in any judicial or administrative proceeding. Such guidelines shall contain specific, descriptive and numeric criteria which will result in a computation of the

support obligation. If the Missouri supreme court does not establish such a rule by October 13, 1989, then each judicial circuit in the state shall by local rule establish such guidelines for use in such circuit. Any rule made pursuant to this subsection shall be reviewed by the promulgating body not less than once every four years to ensure that its application results in the determination of appropriate child support award amounts.

8. Beginning October 13, 1989, there shall be rebuttable presumption, in any judicial or administrative proceeding for the award of child support, that the amount of the award which would result from the application of the guidelines established pursuant to subsection 7 of this section is the correct amount of child support to be awarded. A written finding or specific finding on the record that the application of the guidelines would be unjust or inappropriate in a particular case, after considering all relevant factors including the factors set out in subsection 1 of this section, shall be sufficient to rebut the presumption in the case.

Rule 88 Dissolution, Legal Separation and Child Support

88.01 Presumed Child Support Amount

When determining the amount of child support to order, a court or administrative agency shall consider all relevant factors, including:

(a) the financial resources and needs of the child;
(b) the financial resources and needs of the parents;
(c) the standard of living the child would have enjoyed had the marriage not been dissolved;
(d) the physical and emotional condition of the child; and
(e) the educational needs of the child.

There is a rebuttable presumption that the amount of child support calculated pursuant to Civil Procedure Form No. 14 is the amount of child support to be awarded in any judicial or administrative proceeding for the dissolution of marriage, legal separation, or child support. It is sufficient in a particular case to rebut the presumption that the amount of child support calculated pursuant to Civil Procedure Form No. 14 is correct if the court or administrative agency enters in the case a written finding or a specific finding on the record that the amount so calculated, after consideration of all relevant factors, is unjust or inappropriate.

New Civil Procedure Form No. 14 is hereby adopted to read as follows:

FORM NO. 14 PRESUMED CHILD SUPPORT AMOUNT
CALCULATION OF PRESUMED CHILD SUPPORT AMOUNT
WORKSHEET

	Custodial Parent	Non-Custodial Parent	Combined
1. Monthly gross income:	$_____	$_____	$_____
2. Adjustments:			
a. Other court or administratively ordered child support payments being made	_____	_____	
b. Other spousal support payments being made	_____	_____	
3. Adjusted gross income (Line 1 minus the sum of line 2a and line 2b):	_____	_____	$_____
4. a. Child support obligation (From schedule, using combined gross income from line 3):			$_____
b. Custodial parent's reasonable work-related child care costs:			$_____
5. Combined child support costs (Line 4a plus line 4b):			$_____
6. Proportionate shares of combined income (Each parent's line 3 income divided by line 3 combined income):	_____%	_____%	
7. Each parent's child support obligation (Multiply line 6 and line 4):	_____	_____	
8. PRESUMED CHILD SUPPORT AMOUNT		$_____	

134

Directions For Use

The custodial and noncustodial parent shall calculate the presumed child support amount by completing the worksheet as follows:

Worksheet, line 1

Enter one-twelfth of yearly gross income.

Gross income includes income from any source, except as excluded below, and includes but is not limited to income from salaries, wages, overtime compensation, commissions, bonuses, dividends, severance pay, pensions, interest, trust income, annuities, capital gains, social security benefits, retirement benefits, workers' compensation benefits, unemployment compensation benefits, disability insurance benefits, and spousal support actually received from a person not a party to the order.

For income from rent, royalties, self-employment, proprietorship of a business, or joint ownership of a partnership or closely held corporation, gross income is defined as gross receipts minus ordinary and necessary expenses required to produce income. The court may exclude from ordinary and necessary expenses amounts for depreciation expenses, investments tax credits, and other non-cash reductions of gross receipts. Income, expenses and retained earnings should be reviewed to determine gross income. This amount may differ from a determination of business income for tax purposes.

Income earned from a second job of a sporadic or nonrecurring nature may be included in whole or in part in appropriate circumstances.

Significant employment-related benefits received by a parent may be counted as income.

Exclude from gross income the following: aid to families with dependent children (AFDC) payments; medicaid benefits; supplemental security income (SSI) benefits; food stamps; general assistance benefits; other public assistance benefits having eligibility based on income; and child support received for other children.

135

If either parent is unemployed or underemployed, child support may be calculated in appropriate circumstances based on a determination of potential income. To determine potential income, the court may consider employment potential and probable earnings level based on the parent's recent work history, occupational qualifications, prevailing job opportunities in the community, and whether that parent is custodian of a child whose condition or circumstances make it appropriate that the custodian not be required to seek employment outside the home.

Worksheet, line 2a

Enter the monthly amount of any other court or administrative order for child support from monthly gross income to the extent that such payments are actually being made.

Worksheet, line 2b

Enter the monthly amount of any other court or administrative order for spousal support from monthly gross income to the extent that such payments are actually being made to a person not a party to the action.

Worksheet, line 3

Enter the amount calculated by subtracting from line 1 the sum of the figures entered on line 2a and line 2b. If the result is negative, enter "0."

The combined adjusted gross income is calculated by adding together the adjusted gross income of both parents.

Worksheet, line 4a

Enter the amount determined by use of the attached schedule of basic child support obligations. (See Appendix F -- Schedule of Basic Child Support Obligations, page 143)

Worksheet, line 4b

Enter the reasonable monthly work-related child care costs less any federal income tax credit.

Worksheet, line 5

Enter the amount calculated by adding together line 4a and line 4b.

Worksheet, line 6

Enter the amount calculated by dividing each parent's adjusted gross income (line 3) by the combined adjusted gross income (line 3).

Worksheet, line 7

Enter the amount calculated by multiplying each parent's percentage of combined adjusted gross income (line 6) by the combined child support costs (line 5).

Worksheet, line 8

Enter the amount shown on line 7 for the noncustodial parent.

Comments

No schedule can encompass all of the necessary costs of child rearing or unusual circumstances. The following costs are not included in calculation of the child support amount set forth on the worksheet, line 8.

(A) Health Insurance coverage. For each child support order, consideration should be given to provision of adequate health insurance coverage for the child. See section 452.353, R.S.Mo.

(B) Special needs. Educational expenses such as college, private schools, and tutoring are not factored into the attached schedule. Similarly, extraordinary medical, dental orthodontic, and psychological expenses are not factored into the schedule.

Although in the worksheet a monetary obligation is computed for each parent, the custodial parent is presumed to spend his or her share directly on the child.

Consideration should be given for direct and unreimbursed support provided to a child not the subject of this case, but who is in the custody of one of the parties.

WHO WILL RECEIVE CUSTODY OF THE CHILDREN?

Section 452.375 of the Revised Statutes of Missouri (effective January 1, 1974, amended by legislature 1982, 1983, 1984, 1986, 1988, 1989, 1990) encourages joint legal custody. The section sets out the factors the court is to consider before making a decision concerning custodial arrangements for children:

452.375 Joint legal and joint physical custody defined -- factors determining custody -- public policy of state -- custody options plan, when required -- exchange of information and right to certain records, failure to disclose -- fees, costs assessed, when -- joint custody not to preclude child support -- support, how determined

1. As used in this section, unless the context clearly indicates otherwise:

    (1) "Joint legal custody" means that the parents share the decision-making rights, responsibilities, and authority relating to the health, education and welfare of the child, and, unless allocated, apportioned, or decreed, the parents shall confer with one another in the exercise of decision-making rights, responsibilities, and authority;

    (2) "Joint physical custody" means an order awarding each of the parents significant periods of time during which a child resides with or is under the care and supervision of each of the parents. Joint physical custody shall be shared by the parents in such a way as to assure the child of frequent and continuing contact with both parents.

2. The court shall determine custody in accordance with the best interests of the child. The court shall consider all relevant factors including:

138

(1) The wishes of the child's parents as to his custody;

(2) The wishes of a child as to his custodian;

(3) The interaction and interrelationship of the child with his parents, his siblings, and any other person who may significantly affect the child's best interests;

(4) The child's adjustment to his home, school, and community;

(5) The mental and physical health of all individuals involved, including any history of abuse of any individuals involved;

(6) The needs of the child for a continuing relationship with both parents and the ability and willingness of parents to actively perform their functions as mother and father for the needs of the child;

(7) The intention of either parent to relocate his residence outside the state; and

(8) Which parent is more likely to allow the child frequent and meaningful contact with the other parent.

3.   The general assembly finds and declares that it is the public policy of this state to assure children frequent and meaningful contact with both parents after the parents have separated or dissolved their marriage, and that it is in the public interest to encourage parents to share decision-making rights and responsibilities of child rearing. In order to effectuate this policy, the court shall determine the custody arrangement which will best assure that parents share such decision-making responsibility and authority and such frequent and meaningful contact between the child and each parent, as is indicated in the best interests of the child under all relevant circumstances.

4.   Prior to awarding the appropriate custody arrangement in the best interest of the child, the court shall consider each of the following as follows:

(1) Joint custody to both parents, which shall not be denied solely for the reason that one parent opposes a joint custody award;

(2) Sole custody to either parent; or

(3) Third party custody;

    (a)   When the court finds that each parent is unfit, unsuitable, or unable to be a custodian, or the welfare of the child manifestly demands, and that it is in the best interests of the child, then custody shall be awarded to any other person or persons deemed by the court to be suitable and able to provide an adequate and stable environment for the child. Before the court places custody with a third person under this subdivision, the court shall make that person a party to the action;

    (b)   Under the provisions of this subsection, any person may petition the court to intervene as a party in interest as provided by law.

5.   Unless otherwise decreed, parents are obligated to exchange information with one another concerning the health, education and welfare of the child. In a decree of sole custody, a court may provide that parents shall confer with one another in the exercise of decision-making rights, responsibilities and authority. Upon a finding by the court that either parent has refused to exchange information with one another, which shall include but not be limited to the health, education and welfare of the child, the court shall order the parent to comply immediately and to pay the prevailing party a sum equal to the prevailing party's cost associated with obtaining the requested information, which shall include but not be limited to attorney's fees and court costs.

6.   As between the parents of a child, no preference may be given to either parent in the awarding of custody because of that parent's age, sex, or financial status, nor because of the age or sex of the child.

7.   Any decree providing for joint custody shall include a specific written plan setting forth the terms of such custody. Such plan may be suggested by both parents acting in concert, or one parent acting individually, or if neither of the foregoing occurs, the plan shall be provided by the court. The plan may include a provision

for mediation of disputes in all cases, the joint custody plan approved and ordered by the court shall be in the court's discretion.

8. Unless a noncustodial parent has been denied visitation rights under section 452.400, access to records and information pertaining to a minor child, including, but not limited to, medical, dental, and school records, shall not be denied to a parent because the parent is not the child's custodial parent.

9. If any individual, professional, public or private institution or organization denies access or fails to provide or disclose any and all records and information, including but not limited to past and present dental, medical and school records pertaining to a minor child, to either the custodian or noncustodial parent upon the written request of such parent, the court shall, upon its finding that the individual, professional, public or private institution or organization denied such request without good cause, order that party to comply immediately with such request and to pay to the prevailing party all costs incurred, including but not limited to attorney's fees and court costs associated with obtaining the requested information.

10. An award of joint custody does not preclude an award of child support pursuant to section 452.340. The court shall consider the factors contained in section 452.340 in determining an amount reasonable or necessary for the support of the child.

SCHEDULE OF BASIC
CHILD SUPPORT OBLIGATIONS

Combined Monthly Gross Income	One Child	Two Children	Three Children	Four Children	Five Children	Six Children
100	24	37	46	52	56	60
200	47	73	91	103	112	120
300	71	110	137	155	169	180
400	94	146	183	206	225	240
500	112	174	218	246	268	286
600	129	200	251	283	308	329
700	146	226	283	320	349	372
800	162	253	316	357	389	415
900	179	279	349	394	430	458
1000	196	305	382	431	470	501
1100	210	327	410	463	504	539
1200	223	346	434	490	534	571
1300	235	366	459	517	564	603
1400	248	385	483	544	594	635
1500	260	404	506	570	622	665
1600	271	422	528	595	649	695
1700	282	440	550	620	676	724
1800	293	457	572	645	704	753
1900	305	475	595	671	731	782
2000	318	494	619	698	761	814
2100	330	513	642	725	790	845
2200	343	531	666	752	819	876
2300	355	550	690	779	849	907
2400	368	569	714	806	878	939
2500	380	588	738	833	908	970
2600	392	606	761	859	936	1001
2700	404	625	784	885	965	1031
2800	415	644	808	911	994	1062
2900	427	662	831	937	1023	1092
3000	439	681	855	964	1052	1123

3100	451	700	878	990	1080	1154
3200	463	718	901	1016	1109	1184
3300	474	737	925	1042	1138	1215
3400	486	756	948	1068	1167	1245
3500	498	775	972	1095	1196	1276
3600	508	790	990	1115	1218	1301
3700	516	802	1005	1132	1237	1320
3800	524	814	1020	1149	1255	1340
3900	532	826	1035	1166	1274	1360
4000	540	838	1050	1183	1292	1380
4100	548	850	1065	1201	1310	1399
4200	556	862	1080	1218	1329	1419
4300	564	875	1096	1235	1347	1439
4400	572	887	1111	1252	1366	1458
4500	580	899	1126	1269	1384	1478
4600	588	911	1141	1286	1402	1498
4700	596	923	1156	1303	1421	1517
4800	604	935	1171	1320	1439	1537
4900	612	947	1186	1337	1458	1557
5000	620	959	1201	1354	1476	1577
5100	628	971	1216	1372	1494	1596
5200	636	983	1231	1389	1513	1616
5300	644	996	1247	1406	1531	1636
5400	652	1008	1262	1423	1550	1655
5500	660	1020	1277	1440	1568	1675
5600	668	1032	1292	1457	1586	1695
5700	676	1044	1307	1474	1605	1714
5800	684	1056	1322	1491	1623	1734
5900	692	1068	1337	1508	1642	1754
6000	700	1080	1352	1525	1660	1774
6100	707	1092	1366	1543	1677	1793
6200	713	1101	1378	1556	1691	1808
6300	719	1110	1389	1569	1705	1824
6400	724	1119	1401	1582	1720	1839
6500	730	1128	1413	1595	1734	1854

6600	735	1137	1424	1608	1748	1869
6700	741	1146	1436	1621	1762	1884
6800	747	1155	1447	1634	1776	1900
6900	752	1164	1459	1647	1790	1915
7000	758	1173	1471	1660	1804	1930
7100	763	1182	1482	1673	1818	1945
7200	769	1191	1494	1686	1832	1960
7300	775	1200	1505	1699	1846	1976
7400	780	1209	1517	1712	1861	1991
7500	786	1218	1529	1725	1875	2006
7600	791	1227	1540	1738	1889	2021
7700	797	1236	1552	1751	1903	2036
7800	803	1245	1563	1764	1917	2052
7900	808	1254	1575	1777	1931	2067
8000	814	1263	1587	1790	1945	2082
8100	819	1272	1598	1803	1959	2097
8200	825	1281	1610	1816	1973	2112
8300	831	1290	1621	1829	1987	2128
8400	840	1302	1638	1848	2008	2150
8500	850	1318	1658	1870	2032	2176
8600	860	1333	1677	1892	2055	2202
8700	870	1349	1697	1914	2079	2227
8800	880	1364	1716	1936	2103	2253
8900	890	1380	1736	1958	2127	2278
9000	900	1395	1755	1980	2151	2304
9100	910	1411	1775	2002	2175	2330
9200	920	1426	1794	2024	2199	2355
9300	930	1442	1814	2046	2223	2381
9400	940	1457	1833	2068	2247	2406
9500	950	1473	1853	2090	2271	2432
9600	960	1488	1872	2112	2294	2458
9700	970	1504	1892	2134	2318	2483
9800	980	1519	1911	2156	2342	2509
9900	990	1535	1931	2178	2366	2534
10000	1000	1550	1950	2200	2390	2560

(Adopted October 2, 1989, mandatorily effective April 1, 1990.)

ABOUT THE AUTHOR

Attorney and Mediator--Bill Wear, Jr. has practiced law since 1974 after graduating from the University of Missouri, School of Law. He has practiced law in Honolulu, Hawaii and Kansas City and Springfield, Missouri. He presently practices with his father, Bill Wear, Sr., in the Springfield, Missouri law firm of Wear, Karchmer and Nelms which is the law firm his great grandfather, Hunter Wear, started in 1885. Bill spends most of his time practicing family law (divorce, custody, and grandparents rights) and divorce mediation. He is a member of the following organizations: Missouri Bar Association's Lawyer Assistance Committee and Family Law Section; Hawaii Bar Association's Family Law and Alternative Dispute Resolution Sections; Greene County Bar Association's Family Law Committee; Chairman of the Alternative Dispute Resolution Committee of the Greene County Bar Association and president of the Midwest Mediation Association. Bill also presents mediation trainings that are accredited by the Missouri Bar Association.

Marriage and Family Counselor--Bill has practiced marriage and family counseling since 1978. While living in Hawaii, he was employed as the clinical director of a drug and alcohol treatment center at St. Frances Hospital in Honolulu, Hawaii, worked as an out-patient therapist at the Alcohol Rehabilitation Services of Hawaii and as a family therapist at the Calvary Lutheran Church by the Sea in Aina Hina, Hawaii. He also taught "Ethics" at Antioch University's Graduate School Of Psychology. In addition to his private counseling practice, he teaches classes at Southwest Missouri State University and Forest Institute of Psychology in the areas of interpersonal relationships, mental health and hygiene, divorce mediation and family law. He is a clinical staff member of the Pacific Social Science Institute, a board member of the Ozark Christian Counseling Service, a member of the Ozark Association For Marriage And Family Therapy, Chairman of the Psychiatric Facilities Committee of the Springfield, Missouri Chapter of the Alliance for the Mentally Ill and founding board member of the Springfield, Missouri Chapter of the National Council of Alcoholism. Bill provides staff training for alcohol/drug treatment centers, approved by the American Psychological Association and state licensing authorities for continuing education credit for nurses, professional counselors, therapists, psychologists and physicians.

Minister--Bill graduated from seminary and was ordained in 1987. Bill and his wife Sheila are active in Insight Ministries which is an interdenominational outreach ministry. Bill and Sheila travel throughout the country doing church services and presenting seminars and classes on a variety of subjects including spiritual and emotional healing, "Love, Intimacy and Conflict Resolution", and addiction and co-dependency recovery. Bill is a member of the Ministerial Alliance of the Ozark's Area Council of Churches.

Author--In addition to <u>Recovering From Divorce....and the Horse You Rode In On,</u> Bill has written: "Healing the Wounds of Divorce," "Taking the War Out of Divorce," "Options in Child Custody Litigation," "More Support For Children," and "The Art of Healing Yourself."